DEAR JOHN

Love Letters … from the Wife of an Alcoholic

by MARY GJETSON LEVIN, PH.D.

with the permission of
CATHERINE TURMO FORDE

Forbes
CUSTOM PUBLISHING
60 FIFTH AVE · NEW YORK, NY · 10011

CIP Data is available
Printed in the United States of America
10 9 8 7 6 5 4 3 2 1

ISBN 0–8281–1349–1

TABLE OF CONTENTS

FOREWORD

Mary Gjetson Levin, Ph.D.

I accepted the challenge to write *Dear John* at Catherine Forde's request and after reading her journal. In writing her story, I had two clear advantages that few biographers have. First, I intimately knew the Forde family. Catherine and I were sorority sisters and college roommates at the University of Wisconsin-Madison for two years in the 1960s, and we have remained close friends to this day. Second, I remembered most of the events that she detailed, but from a decidedly different perspective. Her account initially presented a tale filled with anger, hurt, and despair; yet, her expressed reason for writing was to move beyond that torment and on to a new life. I, therefore, asked for permission to reconceptualize her story and to gather additional information from family members and original letters. I chose a first-person, letter format for the text to create a "conversation" between Catherine and John, so long overdue. As if by design, this more introspective account of Catherine's life extinguished her rage, allowing a recognition and an acceptance of her enabling role to emerge. This transformation occurred not only in the text but in Catherine herself, which is the true miracle of *Dear John*.

Each chapter in Part I concludes with John's voice heard through portions of his letters to Catherine, most written from Vietnam. Whereas Catherine reread them over the years to affirm her belief in his goodness, I read them in search of clues that might explain his behavior and that would shed light on Catherine's devotion. In looking for insights, I found a great deal that intrigued me. On the one hand, his letters finally persuaded me that he had been in love, that he had admirable life goals, and that he was capable of empathy. He was planful and frugal and made friends easily. He respected Catherine, yet he was not blind to her vulnerabilities. On the other hand, he assumed (without explicit dialogue on the topic) that his life goals were shared by Catherine, and he believed (also without a conversation on the subject) that he knew how to make her happy. The reader may find it interesting to note the quotations from *The Prophet* by Kahlil Gibran (1963), which John was reading at the time, for they add more than a touch of irony when considered in light of his life's story. How easy it is after the fact to piece together the details of one's life, seeing the strength of patterns and foreshadowing events that almost jump off the page, when examined in retrospect! How difficult it is, by comparison, to see those life designs and to supply those apparent meanings at the time. In other letters, John questions material goals; and he worries about Catherine's character. In the final analysis, I got the distinct impression that he did believe he had all of the answers.

As interesting as these revelations are, even more intriguing are the omissions—the lack of any real commentary, for example, on the war experience itself. One can only speculate as to whether he intentionally withheld information, found talking about it to be too difficult, or was just extremely fortunate in having a relatively uneventful military career. Collectively, John's letters portray a young man who is stable, clear thinking, mature, and devoted. This only makes his life journey more of a mystery, as we are left wondering how a man with such potential could lose his way. Perhaps in his conceit for having all of the answers, he failed to search for the questions that may have served as his guide.

In Part II, I again use Catherine's voice to describe a "12-step program" (to borrow a metaphor) for partners of alcoholics that evolved as *Dear John* began to take shape. I believed that there were valuable lessons for others to learn from Catherine's life story. Together, Catherine and I composed a simple list of suggestions for partners—based upon both her true life experience and my knowledge of scholarly work in the field. I believe that this section of *Dear John*, in particular, speaks persuasively to educators, practitioners, and students specializing in alcohol and other drug addictions. Mental health professionals are most often the ones to whom partners will turn in their search for solutions. They need specific, realistic suggestions—such as those enumerated in Part II—to guide them as they begin their own "recovery" process.

I wish to thank a number of individuals who read early drafts of this manuscript and whose input substantially affected the final version of *Dear John*. First were the Forde children, Kristin, Nels, and Lars, and John's cousin, Lars Swiggum, who corrected perceptions and added rich detail, making the story more true to life. Questions raised by Lee Hawkins, Phyllis Scalia, Lynne Glasman, Esme Gibson, as well as by my sons, David and Chris Finch, provided me with direction for filling in the story's gaps. Throughout this entire project, my husband Joel supplied both the emotional support and the editorial guidance needed to bring *Dear John* to fruition. Without Nick Quint's belief in the validity of this book, it would not have seen the light of day. Finally, I am indebted to

Catherine, who bravely allowed me to assume her voice, to challenge her memory, and to reframe her life. Her generous gift will now be appreciated by many beyond her immediate family and close friends. I am deeply grateful to each of these individuals for their unique contributions.

Mary Gjetson Levin, Ph.D.
Madison, Wisconsin
November 28, 1997

PART I

CATHERINE'S LETTERS

CHAPTER 1

INTRODUCTION

April 21, 1997

Dear John,

My mind races when I try to figure out where to begin this conversation. It has been more than two years since we last spoke and three full *decades* since my letters to you in Vietnam. Gosh, that seems like a lifetime ago! Our letters crossed the Pacific daily for those 12 months. The correspondence helped us both to cope better with the trauma of that separation, and I find myself wanting to write to you now, hoping for similar results. Actually, my therapist suggested that I write to see if it would help release some of this pent-up anger and frustration that I feel. These last two years have been more than difficult, to say the least. I thought that I had already hit bottom years ago, but I seem to have a penchant for misjudging things. You know that I'm really not a writer, John, so you might as well be ready for a few deviations here and there. This would be so much easier if I were painting, when ideas seem to flow from me like melting spring waters preparing their song; but then too much would be left to interpretation, to the "eye of the beholder," as they say. No, I don't want to leave so much to chance, as I may never have the chance again. Let me write, and I will appreciate your forgiving me in advance for any lack of craftsmanship.

I guess I should begin by reassuring you that we are surviving, at times better than at others. You would have been so proud of Kristin last December, receiving her award as one of the top scholars in the University's School of Education. When she graduates next year at the age of 23, she hopes to find a teaching position in an inner city school. She has such compassion for children who do not share equally in all of life's possibilities and is determined to make a difference in their lives. I believe that it is more than that, of course; for I sense that she soothes her own spirit as she reaches out to nurture others. Nels at age 22 is now planning to begin college with hopes of entering some field of business. He found high school a disappointment, never quite meeting his expectations; but you already knew that. He always seemed so much like you, more of a mystery and ever so sensitive; and perhaps he has your entrepreneurial gifts as well. It won't be easy, college, that is. He never really acquired the skills and concentration needed for academic learning while he was in high school. Maybe now when it is on his terms and at his expense, he'll do what needs to be done. And Lars: A more devoted father at the tender age of 20 you could not find anywhere. Shiloh, even at two-and-a-half, is absolutely stunning. She seems to take after my grandmother with her flare for bonnets and ribbons. I know Lars will figure things out; and in the meantime, he's working hard at his job and in school, saving money, and setting some reasonable goals for the first time in his life. As a single parent sharing custody, Lars does not have time for regrets. Yes, music and art will surely figure into his career plans some day. I ache to help him more, but there is little time left for such pleasures or for any kind of giving when there are bills and bills and more bills to pay.

Yes, I suppose I could say that I am making progress, especially if I consider the full distance that I have come and if I can resist the temptation to think about how things might have been. My "Basketree" business even surprises me, to be perfectly honest, because we all know that I don't have a mind for details. People like the product though, so what can I say? I've always been an artist, but you knew that, too. In fact, I think that was probably why you encouraged me to brave this venture in the first place. The appearance is that the enterprise, the kids, and I are doing well; but the reality is far from that. I have enough money to cover day-to-day living expenses, but I struggle to pay off all of the outstanding debts. Your leaving without having paid those years of back taxes (not to mention other damages) resulted in a federal lien, effectively destroying my credit rating for years to come. My hands are tied. I am on my own. I have to believe that I will get past this all someday. If not, I wouldn't be able to go on.

But now I'm getting off the subject. I want to talk about you. Actually, I want to talk about *us* so that I can better understand you. I hope you don't mind if I go back a bit in time to get some perspective. I also hope you don't mind that in my attempt to make this more of a dialogue, I've included a few excerpts from your letters to me—not in chronological order—more thematically arranged. This first one hints at a concern of yours that, quite frankly, I never noticed until now.

Love,

Cathy

Vietnam
August 13, 1967

Dear Cathy,

. . . I'm pretty nostalgic today. I guess because it's Sunday and it just isn't right without you. There isn't a minute that is right without you, but Sunday here is extra slow leaving me too much time to think. I miss you. . . I wish I could be with you to at least try to make you happy. If I get nothing else out of being here, I do know that what I want most from life is to make you happy. . . Maybe after being here I will be better at it. I sometimes can't believe, or understand why, you are willing to wait all this time for me. Love is a funny thing. . . I thank God for it and for you.

ja elska da ["I love you" in Norwegian]

John

CHAPTER 2

THE LEGACY OF OUR YOUTH

The Normalization of Alcohol

April 23, 1997

Dear John,

There was a time when you did make me happy, happier than I ever could have dreamed to be. Do you remember when we first met? I realize, of course, that this is a rhetorical question; but I've asked it to jog your memory a bit. I want to start there and go back even further if I can, because I want us to remember the good times—those happy times—how it was that I fell in love with you, and what it was about your childhood that both intrigued and puzzled me. I knew from the beginning, as everyone else seems to have known, that we were so very different in the manner of our upbringing, a contrast that I always maintained made us perfect complements. I can admit now what I could not have known at the time, that I fell in love with you and everything about you because I was ready to fall in love and you were there. It certainly helped that you were tall and handsome, a Norwegian Lutheran through and through (as I was), and an incredible vocalist who appreciated my interests in the graphic arts. I didn't mind that you enjoyed your cigarettes and beer, actually rather common pleasures for teenagers and college students in the '60s. You were a gentleman, a romantic, fun, intelligent, a lover of good music and off-the-road restaurants, a reader of popular novels and newsy periodicals; and you were attracted to me.

The Year was 1964

I remember as if it were yesterday when we first said hello in that huge Geology 101 lecture the spring semester of our freshman year. It was the snow-crunching-cold January of 1964. I remember the precise date because it was right after the Beatles first appeared on "Ed Sullivan," and everyone was still talking about them. I was late for class, as became my habit. You were sitting in the very last row and concentrating intently on the professor's first-day remarks.

"Excuse me," I said, hoping to get your attention so that I could take the only vacant seat remaining, which happened to be next to you. "Excuse me," I said a bit louder, meaning "I'd like to take that seat, if you don't mind. Please let me through."

Finally you looked up and whispered, "Oh, I'm sorry," as you flipped down the writing table from the arm of your seat so that I could squeeze by with my awkward, doesn't-fit-anywhere drawing portfolio in tow.

"Thank you. Did I miss anything yet?" I asked.

"No, not really," you answered without actually looking at me, and that was it: our very first "conversation."

I was never really interested in terminal moraines or fault lines, but very soon I began to take a definite interest in you. There were no assigned seats in that class. Nevertheless, we sat in the very same places day after day, last row on the right-hand side, first two seats from the aisle. I always seemed to be late and out of breath, having run down the sidewalk on Observatory Drive from my art lab (you must remember that hanger-shaped Quonset hut behind the Education Building) to the front entrance of Science Hall and up the marble steps, arriving finally at Lauden's famous first-floor lecture theater. I loved that room with those huge, south-facing arched windows, framing the tops of elms and oaks that bordered Bascom Hill. Soon my routine became familiar to you, I knew, because you'd wait to pull up your writing table until after I arrived.

We didn't really interact much. You conscientiously took pages of notes, while I attended to my renderings of intrusive rock formations and the like. Then suddenly and uncharacteristically you were absent for several lectures in a row. "Well, you're back!" I said upon first seeing you again. "I thought that maybe you'd dropped this course."

"No, actually I was in the hospital," you offered with no further explanation. Later you said that it was due to some sort of respiratory problem or whatever.

"Listen. You're welcome to use my notes," I said, feeling somewhat embarrassed about their lacking in sufficient detail. "At least you'll know what topics we covered."

"Thanks. Maybe I will." Again, that was it—no big conversation. After class, I handed you my notebook, figuring that was the end of that. I don't mean to imply that the only reason for offering you my notes was to get a date. I was already dating a few different guys. I was concerned about you. You seemed to be such a serious student, and I imagined that you'd be worried about how to catch up. I guess that would be the beginning of a pattern of my wanting to help you, a pattern that continued for years to come in one form or another. Funny, isn't it, how things get started?

You must have felt good about my gesture because it was shortly afterwards that you did call to ask me out for a date. I don't even remember exactly what we did that first night—probably went to one of those crowded campus bars with tile floors still sticky from last night's spilled beer—someplace where we could sit and talk. Anyway, that evening eventually led to more dates; and as spring finals began to approach, we talked about our plans for summer. You were going back to help your dad on the farm, and I told you about my getting a job in southern Wisconsin as a camp art counselor. Suddenly it occurred to both of us that the summer was going to be painfully long, which eventually led to your decision to pay me a week-long visit. That visit changed the entire course of my life. Really, there is nothing quite like an evening swim in a sun-warmed lake rimmed with pine trees under a sky sprinkled with quadrillions of stars. I remember, too, our midnight walks with stories about your farm. I couldn't believe that you would drive all the way across the entire state of Wisconsin just to see me. That alone made me ache to know you more. Yes, I had my share of boyfriends in high school; but none had ever held my heart until you, John; and it happened during that summer of 1964.

Let me be the first to admit, as I look back with clearer vision, that I was desperately in need of an escape from my home and our too-clean, upper-middle-class neighborhood of Wauwatosa. Your peaceful, endearing rural life on Nash Ridge near the Mississippi—complete with its picturesque white farmhouse in the valley surrounded by green meadows and hillside forests—that life, John, seduced me, comforted me, convinced me that we were meant for each other. It didn't seem to matter that only your father had graduated from high school. Your parents had such a simple, yet happy life. During my sister Liz's wedding after camp that August, I dreamed silently—completely to myself—of walking down the aisle with you one day. It was all so perfect in my mind. You were perfect. I was perfectly happy. We were a perfect couple. I have wondered over the years, though, what it was that attracted you to me.

My family was so different from yours in almost every way. My Brooklyn-born father, the son of a small-town minister, successfully rose through the ranks of a large Milwaukee company. Mom was a wonderful and most creative mother—entirely responsible for some of my dearest childhood memories of joyous Christmases and magical birthday parties. Her father had been a wealthy Wisconsin merchant (who later lost his share of the family fortune—but that's another story). Both of my parents had college degrees. We lived in the suburbs, vacationed in big cities and at northern Wisconsin resorts. We were a family that was comfortably, although not extremely, well off.

Appearances aside, a dark cloud seemed to hang over my family. The Turmos and Torrisons were groomed for silence when it came to personal matters, so I am probably violating the family charter by admitting on paper that virtually every adult relative whom I can remember drank to excess. I don't think that my brother or sister was any more aware of the alcohol, or less troubled by it, than I was. In fact, we simply accepted it as normal. Heavy drinking was a way of life among most of the people we knew, family for sure and friends of our parents as well. Weddings turned into full-blown cocktail parties, cocktail parties grew into evenings of chaos, and quiet evenings of conversation slid into nonsense and sleep. The sound of kitchen cupboard doors slamming and slamming and slamming downstairs after dad went to bed still echoes in my mind. Why mom became so full of rage was a mystery to me at the time, although I think that I understand better now. It never felt good though, even if it were normal. I couldn't have told you why then. I can now; but as I said before, my vision is clearer. I wanted a life that was genuine, wholesome, and pure. I grew up surrounded by alcohol and all of the pretenses that went with it; and, John, *you* were my ticket out.

I still haven't answered my own question, have I? Why were you attracted to me? Did you see the wealth and miss the alcohol? Was it the "off-beat style," as my roommate Mary used to claim, in reference to my dancer's posture and consignment-store clothes? It definitely was not my intellect, for a gifted student I never claimed to be. I guess I was kind of attractive in a disorganized sort of way. Kristin inherited my natural curly, blonde hair and wears it sometimes as I did—all piled on top of her head, a few loose tendrils wisping in the breeze and held in place by a couple of randomly placed bobbi pins. That casually combed, somewhat frazzled hair was perfect for those long beaded earrings we all used to wear with turtleneck sweaters, antique necklaces, flouncy skirts, and boots. Suffice it to say that I was not exactly the knee socks, kilt, and circle-pin type!

I know you enjoyed our sorority "combo" where I was dressed as a hillbilly farmer's wife, singing harmony and keeping the beat on an old scrub board with a stiff wire brush. Then there were the Langdon Street ice-carving contests, which Barb and I worked on through the night, winning first place for three years straight. I did get called into action for those kinds of projects as one of the few art majors in our sorority, designing floats for Homecoming, creating sets for that all-Greek fund-raiser, *Humorology,* and even getting a commission for a painting to hang in the living room of our house. But all of this was later—after our dating became serious the following year. I told you about my career ambition, to become a teacher, and about my love of everything creative: art galleries, concerts, good movies, gardens, dance, folk singing, and plays. I wanted to make the world more beautiful. I wanted to make a difference. I was confident that once on my own, I could do just that. We shared these kinds of thoughts and aspirations as a means of getting a "barometer reading" on each other's future possibilities. These are still my goals, still my dreams. That much I have always known.

I suppose it doesn't make any difference at this point to know exactly how I might have captured your attention, but it is fun to try to guess. It is a way of attempting to know that very secret part of you that you always seemed afraid to let me see. I wish I had asked you many more things so that I could have known you better. I realized too late, of course, that there were a great number of unknowns. You were much more complicated than you first appeared; but then again, so was I.

Your childhood, John, remains an enigma to me to this very day. On the one hand, it seemed so idyllic—your one-room school house, early mornings milking the cows, long solitary bareback rides down dusty country roads—just like in the movies. On the other hand, you talked in later years about being alone so much of the time, living a very isolated sort of life. Your farm was miles from the nearest neighbor, much less the nearest friend. Interrupting the loneliness during those quiet times were the many farm chores for which you were responsible, work that always came before play. Maybe you saw me as *your* ticket out. Isn't that incredible, that maybe each of us was looking for a kind of happiness that we thought the other possessed?

It strikes me as amazing even now as I stop to think that your father was 55 years old when you were born, probably not much of a companion as you grew up, and perhaps increasingly dependent on you as he grew older. I still can see those porcelain-blue eyes set deeply under thick white brows and that rough, expressionless face heavily wrinkled and all-knowing. He was striking, commanding; but I wondered how at the age of 73 he experienced bringing you to the University. He appeared to be more like a grandfather when I first met him, walked proudly but with a slower gait. Somehow, I don't think that other people's thoughts or judgments on the subject mattered to him. That's just a guess on my part, but I certainly don't remember your saying anything to the contrary. He was the prototypical Norwegian: rarely displaying any emotion, seldom engaging in lengthy conversation, reluctant to share any of his thoughts or even to show his love for you in a demonstrative sort of way. Still, he had an inner strength and quiet presence that everyone felt when he entered the room.

I was so glad that you were able to recall his touch, a gesture so unusual for him, when he reached out to protect you as you began to cross a busy street in town one Saturday afternoon. It is amazing, isn't it, how such a small moment like that can take on such important meaning in one's life? You knew that he loved you from that time on, in spite of how resistant he seemed about letting you know; and you talked about replaying that single scene in your mind so many times—your stepping off the curbing to cross the street, his noticing a pickup truck speeding toward you, and then his large hand reaching out suddenly, fingers spread apart totally covering your small chest and holding you back firmly, tenderly, safely—but never voicing a single word of caution or reprimand. I could be reading more into this event than it deserves, but it seems to mirror so much of our life together. I, too, have memories of similar moments that we shared, convincing me that you really did love me, John, even though you kept your distance so much of the time. Others might believe that I am grasping at straws, but I'll get back to that later. I'm getting side-tracked again, of course. I was talking about your childhood.

I'll have to be honest here and tell you that I am inferring some of this from bits and pieces of conversations we had over the years, from some of my very few talks with your sister, and from your mother when she forgot to tighten her lip. It always seemed somewhat strange to me. No one in your family had much to say about anything, at least not when I was around, almost appearing secretive at times; but that really wasn't it. I imagined that perhaps your father was more comfortable speaking in Norwegian because he subscribed to a weekly Norwegian newspaper, remember? I hadn't even realized that there were foreign language papers available and had no idea why people would want to read in their old languages. I know he could read English. After all, he was a high school graduate. Your mother, however, completed only the eighth grade. More important was the 25-year difference in your parents' ages! Now you'll have to agree; that was unusual! Your parents made a living; but not much more, kept purse money for special occasions in a sugar bowl on the top shelf of the kitchen cupboard, and got indoor plumbing for the first time after you were born. There were few family vacations, other than day trips to visit nearby relatives and your favorite cousin Lars—after the cows were milked, of course. Perhaps your parents believed that these humble beginnings and their simple life left nothing more to be said. I don't know, but I have wondered about that more than once.

What I did learn during our many visits to the farm over the years was that life in your community centered on the church, and life in your family centered on you. All social events were held at the church—weddings, funerals, ice cream socials—with every neighbor, teacher, and family member in attendance. Making your parents' world just that much brighter, of course, were your musical talents and academic accomplishments. Do you realize that I never heard you play the tuba? Those trophies and ribbons were evidence enough that you were far above average, which didn't really surprise me because your mother had been telling me so for years. Yes, you were the pride of your high school, your music teacher's star pupil, the valedictorian of your class; but all of that pales when I think of you singing.

I'm not just saying this, John, really I'm not. Your voice, that rich baritone, was absolutely extraordinary. I just wish that audio tapes were available in those days so that the children and I could enjoy those concerts on the Mississippi River, the seasonal school recitals, the church solos on Sundays, even your family singing at home around the old piano. We thankfully still have a very amateurish recording made many years ago, although I'll have to admit that the words ring a bit too true and painful for listening to now. "Ol' Man River:" I know you remember it, sort of your signature piece. You loved to sing it, and it was the perfect song for you. I have often wondered if you were trying to tell us all something through your singing of that song specifically, something you could not talk about in plain conversation, perhaps about your fears or your view of life. For you, John—and not unlike your father, I might add—it was always so difficult to talk about things close to your heart, yet so easy to find your release through music.

You'd be happy to know how many people remember you to this day in part because of your voice. Isn't that amazing, with all that you achieved as a state lobbyist, that what people remember with perfect clarity and immediate pleasure is John singing? Religious hymns that touched the entire congregation at our country church in DeForest, love songs for your Delta Gamma sweetheart at the sorority house in college, sentimental favorites like "Edelweiss" when family or friends begged for just one more, and familiar country ballads in one of those road-side taverns with the guys. You were gifted, pure and simple. What was the name of that foursome of yours in college where you sang and played a bass fashioned out of an old washtub and broom stick? The Foggy Mountain Boys, I think it was, with Chuck and Jim and Bob. Anyway, the four of you were asked to perform all over campus, in your blue-jean overalls and plaid-flannel shirts, always singing with a characteristic country drawl in perfect harmony. You had so many musical gifts, really, and that is one reason it has been difficult for me to accept your life decisions.

Your mother still remembers you, I am sure, as you were in high school; and she fills with pride, I am also sure, when she thinks back to those standing ovations during competitive events and the thunder of applause that followed your concerts. Your talents rewarded the entire family with a special status it could not have achieved otherwise. I wonder if your parents ever really showed their appreciation to you or expressed their pride in any other way. It seemed to me that they just wore the stole themselves. I could be wrong, but your parents' love seemed to you to have been conditional to some extent. You never ceased to try to understand their reserve. Your mother's tendency to burst into tears when things didn't go as she preferred made you guard every thought, filter every word before daring to speak—even all these years after you left the farm. Your father's only comment to you as a teenager was, "That's your mother," never offering an explanation for behavior that seemed to you to be disturbingly strange. Maybe he just meant for you to accept her, not to try to change her, or to ask any more questions. Well, nobody is perfect. They did their best. It's not like we can do anything about it at this point anyway.

Okay, I know you get embarrassed by this kind of picture. It would probably be more accurate to say that you were a typical teenager in many respects, not the least of which was due to your favorite high school pastimes: hanging out, smoking and having a few beers with the guys (the staples of your every teenage social gathering), your love of cars (their horse power and cylinder count), and girls and cards (playing games with both, from what I can tell). I wonder, however, whether your friends read as much as you did, whether you shared with them your fascination with novels and philosophy and news. Or were those just secret passions? You discussed your readings in practically every letter you sent from overseas, asking me to keep sending best-seller books while you subscribed to periodicals such as The *Wall Street Journal* on your own. Clearly, literature and learning were not merely passing pleasures.

No one knew you better nor shared more time with you during those early, formative years than your cousin Lars. That doesn't mean that he was any less confused by your inner self than the rest of us. On the contrary, he still puzzles over your favorite, conversation-stopping interjection—"I know all of the answers. I just don't know the questions."—and the book that absolutely captivated you: *Advise and Consent*, about power, power people, and power strategies to win at life's games. Just months younger, he always felt himself to be in your shadow, but that wasn't such a bad place to be. He glowed with pride in watching you soar to heights unknown to most people from Nash Ridge. That connection, that feeling of brotherhood that came on both of your parts from a genuine love, survives to this very day.

And what about me? It's only fair, I guess, to review a few more details about my own pre-college years, things that you didn't know for many years to come. It helps me to put this on paper, even if it seems so much a part of the past, because it places our subsequent life together in a broader context. My family legacy remains to this day a driving force in my life, as you well know.

I came from a family primarily comprised of two distinct kinds of individuals: alcoholics and eccentrics.

As ridiculous as it may sound though, life was always exciting. You'll have to agree that people who drink can be a lot of fun. They like parties, tell great jokes, mingle with everyone, and unlike their more sober counterparts, seem to be carefree and full of life. The eccentrics added the style, and the one who embodied those "elements of style" to the n-th degree was my grandmother. Gramma Torrison rarely entered a room without some kind of cape flung over her shoulders, a flamboyant brimmed hat tilted at just the right angle, and those elbow-length gloves of hers smothered with silver bracelets. She could strike a pose anywhere, whether standing near a sweeping staircase or a chain-link fence, always looking like someone who stepped right out of *Vogue* magazine. It goes without saying that my grandmother might have had a tough time living a common, country life.

Mom inherited the same sense of flare, although tempered a bit over the years by her more Republican surroundings. I wish I had seen her childhood home in Manitowoc with those red-velvet curtains, the baroque furniture, and the spectacular chandelier that hung in the front hallway. Mom always talked about that house, with those magnificent images coming to mind along with the fragrances of freshly cut flowers and coffee brewing—completing what must have been a perfect masterpiece. She actually spent more time in Chicago as a child, where they moved after her father's economic collapse, but prefers to drop that subject and those times that ended so shamefully with his death from some kind of alcohol-related disease. Always a "quick study," she acquired a keen sense of taste and design from her "Windy City" walks past glamorous, store-front window displays. Those "educational" opportunities paid off well in later years after marrying Dad and when she actually could afford to shop for the very first time.

I clearly remember our looking forward to family gatherings, certain of some kind of side-show from one of the clan. You probably remember that episode at my cousin Lynn's wedding. I know I told you. She was the one who graduated from Arizona State University, married a handsome man of Mexican descent (much to my Aunt Mary's horror—but again, that is another story). Anyway, her father-in-law-to-be was not able to come to the wedding due to a serious illness, which absolutely infuriated Lynn's mother. It gets worse, of course. Aunt Mary received word in the middle of the rehearsal dinner—talk about timing!—that he had just passed away. The room became completely silent with all eyes focused in her direction, waiting for the inevitable response. And how did she respond? With pained sympathy or even insincere concern? Not Aunt Mary! Her only remark, spoken above the hush and with not a small element of disdain: "You'd think the bastard could have waited until next week!" You had to be there, I know, to appreciate the image of her tripping and twirling around in her spike heels, size 4, and red-chiffon dress, martini in hand, "three sheets to the wind." Well, John, you can probably see why your simple country life appealed to me. I just wanted something less piercing, more serene.

I don't want to go into all of the gory details. We've had enough of our own. The short version of my family story is that too many of my aunts and uncles died tragically in alcohol-related events. I recall car accidents, illnesses, suicides, cancers, heart attacks—you name it. You were there to see so much of this with me, attending one funeral after another while we were in college. We both could see how alcohol abuse led to these tragic endings. None who drank as they did seemed able to escape some kind of awful outcome. Why didn't we respond earlier to our own problem? Couldn't we see the pattern repeating itself? Well, John, perhaps someone without my kind of family history would have been better able to confront you and your drinking. I surely wasn't the person for that job. I was more equipped to put up with it, at any cost, just as did my aunts, great aunts, mother, grandmother, and great-grandmother before me. And you'll have to admit that like them, I was rather good at it.

Then there were those college years. The University of Wisconsin, you surely would agree, was not just any college campus. Ours had a national reputation for drinking and partying well before we arrived and an even stronger reputation for pot and protesting by the time our decade of the '60s ended. I vaguely recall some poll that was reported in *Playboy* magazine, which ranked the country's top party schools. The UW was not even on the list, but then there was an asterisk directing the reader to a footnote that read something like: "The University of Wisconsin was not included in this survey. We didn't believe it was fair to rank the amateurs with the professionals." That was where we came of age, John—the place and the time. Adding to it were our independent decisions to join the Greek system where beer was center stage every Friday and Saturday night.

I found the drinking to be appalling at first, perhaps because I never drank in high school. Soon even I became rather comfortable with both drinking and smoking, although to be perfectly honest (and I know you would agree), I never had more than one or two. I could sip on a single glass of beer for hours. It gave me a kind of euphoria, a confidence, an illusion of having arrived. It seemed so adult—as long as I was under control, which I am certain I always managed to be—to sit on a bar stool with a cigarette in one hand and a beer in the other. I rather liked that image, actually. It felt even more adult with you, however, during our sophomore year when you had your apartment. We'd go back alone after a day of classes, and I'd make you dinner. We'd have a drink, relax, and then—well, you know the rest.

I was already so head-over-heels in love with you when I came back to school that September. My classes seemed totally irrelevant to the more important thing on my mind—which, of course, was you. The fact that you would make that 6-hour drive just to see me at camp was all the evidence that I needed to know that you were in love with me, too. It was so easy for those quiet evenings of studying together in your apartment to transition into more intimate matters. I doubt that I ever told you, John, but for me the decision to let you make love to me that fall was a part of my secret decision to marry you. Afterwards for me, there was no turning back. Yes, I know that your proposal didn't come for more than two years. That didn't matter to me at the time. I just knew that eventually you would want to marry me, too. I was brought up in a very strict religious family, where no one did these things outside of marriage. I created my own minor exception to the rule, however, to deal with my love for you and the guilt that followed: "It" was okay, I reasoned, as long as we *intended* to be married someday. That was my plan, if you want to know the actual truth. I am admitting it for the first time now—here—in this letter to you. For me, marriage was a given. I thought (hoped) it was for you, too. I was so completely, positively, absolutely in love. Nothing else mattered. Does this make sense?

The hematite pin encircled with silver, the peaceful weekends on the banks of the Mississippi and the ridges of Crawford county, fall festivals with bar-b-qued chicken, and fresh farm breakfasts: Who would not have fallen in love with your world and with you? It is somewhat of a fantasy to me even now; and yet I can see it so clearly, too. We must have gone back to the farm dozens of times during those undergraduate years and in the first years after we were married. John, do you remember your father playing the violin, with me accompanying him on the piano? I loved those times more than I ever told you, and I loved you even more. I wanted this for the rest of my life and was certain that you did, too. I was willing to pledge my whole self to you no matter what, and I did. The only reason that I mention this, John, is that I have occasionally wondered why I did remain so bonded to you, so faithful to you, and why I didn't let myself become even the slightest bit serious about anyone else ever again. As ridiculous as it may sound in this day and age, I just couldn't imagine how I could be with anyone else after I had already been with you.

Summer and Fall of 1965

I might have been more concerned about your thoughts on the subject, however, for there were no camp visits and few letters from you during the summer of '65. That absence of attention, almost a lack of interest on your part, I chose to ignore for whatever reason, something that I seem to have done throughout our marriage. I do remember that you said you "totaled" the family car in August during a rather serious alcohol-related accident—with your cousin, I think it was. But what were you doing that whole first week when we returned to school that September? I, who hadn't seen you for most of the summer, waited by the phone literally for five straight days, while my new roommate Mary—who hardly knew me then—tried to cheer me up. It seems that she has been trying to cheer me up for 35 years! Your stock value dropped more than a few points in her book right from the start, and it plummeted completely a few months later. I didn't really care what she thought. I was not ready to listen to a rational argument.

I was glad when we resumed dating that fall and even more thrilled in December when you gave me your fraternity pin. The surprise event (usually regarded as a pre-engagement commitment, at least by the girls) by tradition took place with both houses present, men and women, and late at night at the sorority house. Only our Housemother was informed that a pinning would happen so that she could unlock the front door. When the familiar bell was rung, all of the girls came downstairs, not knowing whose pinning it would be. The ceremony required the young man to sing his fraternity's sweetheart song. I still get chills recalling that moment when I heard your then familiar voice and realized that this pinning ceremony would be mine. Your brothers hummed to accompany you, none in the room ever having heard you sing solo before that moment. I looked around at my sisters and saw not a single dry eye. You captured all of their hearts, not just mine, and were unanimously elected a few days later as the "DG Man" for our Christmas formal. Everyone, even Mary, began to see in you what I had known all along. It felt like we were truly a "couple." I began to believe that my secret wish, made for the first time during Liz's wedding more than a year before, might actually come true. That is why, John, when you started to date other women the next semester, it just tore me to pieces.

January to October of 1966

Within two months of that pinning, you announced to me that it was over. You thought that we should date other people, that we had been together for so long, and that it might be a good idea to see if we would miss each other. "Then we would really know," you stated without so much as a hint of passion.

"Really know?" I asked myself, as if we needed proof. I already *really* knew, and I was devastated! Not being able to think of anything to say that would change your mind, I cried. Obviously, that didn't work either. I wondered why we got pinned in the first place, if you really didn't want to. Did you feel pressured to do so? Was breaking up some kind of test for me, to find out if I really did love you? I do know that being pinned was definitely what I wanted. Anyway, after we broke up, Mary was ready to kill me every time the phone rang.

"Hello. . . . No, this is Mary. . . . You want to speak with Cathy?. . . Just a minute. I'll see if she's down the hall." Then covering the phone, she'd yell, "Caaaaathy!" She'd look at me curled up on the bed, the blanket pulled up to my chin, and whisper, "Well, are you here or not?"

"Who is it?" I'd ask.

"Sounds like Bob, maybe Dave. I don't know. Who cares! It's a guy! Why don't you just talk to him?" she'd beg.

I'd frown and pull the blanket up to my eyes, shaking my head from side to side. Mary would gasp in complete frustration.

"I guess she's not here," she'd say after the right amount of time. "No, I'm not sure when she'll be back, maybe after 10:00. . . . Yes, I'll tell her you called. . . . Bye." Then she'd hang up, turn to face me with one hand on her hip and her eyes in that squint of hers, which demanded an explanation.

"Why did you say after 10:00?" I'd ask.

"You've got to do something," she'd say. "You can't just lie around here waiting for John forever. He's out having a great time! And what are you doing? Nothing. . . week after week! There are tons of guys who want to go out with you. You know, Cathy, it wouldn't kill you to say 'yes' to one of them one time—if even to show John a thing or two."

"You just don't understand," I'd say.

"I don't have to be a rocket scientist to understand that you need to get out of that bed," she'd declare in her know-it-all tone of voice; and then she'd pace. (I hated this part.) "Nine out of 10 of these phone calls are for you. Do you realize that? Get over that jerk! He doesn't deserve you! You should be treated better than that! Just exactly how long are you going to wait, Cathy? Oh, I give up!" Finally, she'd relent and go back to her desk. I didn't have to be a genius either to understand that she was completely exasperated.

Out of total desperation one afternoon, she dragged out a red satin cape that Grandma Torrison had given me for my twenty-first birthday with the companion black-ribboned hat. She costumed herself and put on some show tunes, dancing around the room—cane in hand—impersonating everyone from Marilyn Monroe to Liza Minelli, trying to make me laugh and to get me out of the full-blown depression into which I had sunk. It worked and brings a smile to my face even now when I think about it. I had to pull myself out of it, if not for me, then for her. At the end of that day, we (she, really) decided to take a somewhat passive-aggressive stance and arranged to have a dead Easter lily sent to you at the Beta House as a not-so-subtle message that you were about to be "history!" That *did* feel good, I'll have to admit, silly as it sounds. And evidently, it did get your attention.

I never did get over you, John, after we broke up that winter, even with Mary's entertaining and prodding and plotting. You seemed determined to help me do exactly that with all of your partying and dating, about which everyone was convinced I needed to know. Do you see a theme building here? I never gave up on you no matter what you did, ever. I was still too in love. When you did come back late that spring, I was only too ready for you, although absolutely no one understood my decision.

"Cathy, what are you doing?" Bev asked in a tone that really said, "Are you an idiot?"

"Don't worry. I think I can handle this. I'll give him just one more chance," I said, trying to reassure her that if you broke up with me again, that was it. "We might make it, you know. I have to find out."

"*Might* make it! Is *might* good enough for you?" Esme jumped in. "Every time you walk into a room,

Cathy, guys' heads turn. Aren't you even curious about who else is out there?"

"Look, Cathy. At least consider making him wait," Lea recommended. "Don't appear so anxious. Make him sweat!"

"Have a cigarette," Tina offered, with the two of us then taking the much-needed draw of nicotine in unison. "So, Catherine, you think you're making a wise decision?" she queried me.

"What about telling him to jump. . . ." When Mary started in again, I just walked out of the room. Thank heavens for cigarettes, or I'd never have survived those inquisitions. I couldn't listen to any of them. I couldn't undecide what I had already decided the previous year in your apartment. There was no going back. I never seriously dated anyone else again, although I do remember Bob and Dave, in particular. Both were from well-established families, were ready for a committed relationship; and we did go out a few times. The question remained nevertheless: How could I ever "be" with them, when I had given my heart, my everything, to you?

We had so little time to renew our relationship and to get back on solid ground, a couple of weeks at most before you left for your summer job on the railroad and I began summer school. You never did give me an adequate explanation for our breakup. You talked instead about how much you had missed me, how it drove you crazy to think about my going out with other guys, and how you had to be with me again. I was so happy to have you back that I didn't ask for explanations or for justifications. I had missed you terribly. The summer separation was ill-timed and in no way prepared me for the longer separation to come. It did help somewhat to correspond. Never in any of your letters that summer—and I still have those letters, John—did you tell me about your flunking out of school from all of that playing and partying; and then, about your being eligible for the draft! I couldn't even process it. You were nearly a straight-A student. How could you just stop going to class? What I also cannot understand in hindsight is why you didn't tell me these critically significant details. These were rather serious omissions on your part, even as I think about it now. Were you afraid I'd drop you, especially after your breakup with me? Even more curious is why I didn't even seek an explanation. Was I afraid to ask, fearing that you might drop *me*? I guess I'd just like to have some answers so that I can put this, along with so many other details from the past, to rest.

I wish I had considered the significance of this deception more when I returned to school at the end of August. Perhaps I would have been more cautious; but I focused instead on your destiny, Vietnam, and on my impending loneliness without you. There were times that were especially hard in the sorority house that fall, like when we'd all gather in the living room to sing folk songs before dinner. The more musically talented girls took turns playing their guitars, and we'd sing the favorites from the Kingston Trio, Joan Baez, the Mamas and the Papas, the New Christy Minstrels—those familiar songs with easy melodies that everyone knew. It was a "'60s kind of thing" to gather spontaneously in groups like that to sing. It gave us feelings of comfort and togetherness while street demonstrations, civil rights marches, sit-ins, and protests punctuated the rest of our days. Ours was a campus that lived those struggles not from a distance but up-close.

Eventually, the girls would get to "Where have all the flowers gone?" and to the Peter, Paul, and Mary ballad—I forget the name—anyway it had the lyrics: "Johnny, oh Johnny, I know you have to go. Won't you let me go with you?". . . "No, my love, no." Everyone would become completely absorbed in the beautiful melodies and harmonies or on someone's solo along the way. It was soulful fiction to them, but it was happening to me. I can still see it all so clearly in my mind's eye—all of us gathered around to sing as Kay strummed on her guitar, my sitting on a chair near Mary who was seated cross-legged on the carpet, her glancing up at me when she realized those words were hitting too close to my real life experience, and then seeing my tears well and my throat tighten preventing any sound from coming, while she pondered again how to help me. Why do I know what she was thinking? She told me only recently about having almost the identical image frozen in her memory as well. She sensed correctly that my biggest fear was your safety and my greatest nightmare was that you might not be coming home at all. I managed to keep these thoughts to myself—or at least I thought so until now.

You probably don't even remember, do you, about passing out that night in October of 1966 before you left for basic training? I saw you very little that fall, but we had arranged a last romantic weekend together in Madison before you were to leave. You must have been thinking only about yourself, perhaps afraid or at least apprehensive about what was to come. That makes perfect sense to me now. Of course you would be worried about what was going to happen! The daily papers and evening news were filled with brutal images of dead bodies and the horrors of a war that seemed to be going nowhere. I didn't think about that for some reason. I was really thinking about myself and what was to become of me. I wondered about whether you really cared for me, whether you thought about how this would affect me, whether you knew how much I worried. As I write all of this to you now, I wonder whether I even tried to tell you. I wanted you to know it without my having to tell you. I can't recall our discussing anything specific about our future, for example, or even about whether there would actually be a future. You never asked me to wait for you, nor did you say that you'd wait for me. I also wonder whether I ever let you talk to me about your fears or if we both just pushed those feelings out of mind. They were pretty difficult for 21-year-olds to handle. We didn't know how to talk then, or later. I guess I believed that you felt as I felt. I never even thought about asking if it were true.

It is amazing how letters helped us survive the long months of training and service ahead. I have to say, your letters were beautiful. They gave me strength to endure the loneliness and affirmed in me all of the wonderful feelings I had about you. I saved them all, as I said before. If the house is burning down and I have a chance to grab only a few precious possessions, the shoe box with your letters will be among the first items I choose. I have always believed they revealed the real you, or the you I knew you could be. John, I must confess that I always wished you could just say those kinds of things to me in person. You never did. We never talked about our future, our dreams, whether we would have children, the kind of life we wanted. Maybe we assumed that we wanted the same things.

January to December of 1967

You left for training during my senior year shortly before I left Madison for Milwaukee to complete my student teaching. I moved back home with my parents that spring semester, feeling very distant in more ways than one from my friends at the University. Their lives with boyfriends and social activities were continuing as usual—so predictable, so certain; and ours was not. I surely couldn't see myself participating in any anti-war demonstrations when soon you would be going to Vietnam. I got through those paralizingly lonely times with the help of your letters, which convinced me that we were falling deeply in love. When you came home in the spring, after training, I knew. When you asked me to marry you, I accepted. Too quickly, those feelings of joy were displaced by fear and abandonment, as I watched you board the plane at Milwaukee's Mitchell Field for Vietnam. I had become dependent on you for my happiness, my well-being, my future. How could we survive apart for 12 more months? My engagement ring with your promise of marriage became my salvation, but it was still so difficult. I couldn't imagine that there would ever be a more traumatic time in my life than that painfully long year of separation with you at least 50 zillion miles away.

I dealt with the pain by sending you letters and packages, hundreds of them, probably more than any 300 "army widows" combined. And, John, you wrote back whenever you had a chance, almost every day.

Your letters told me how you were feeling, what you had experienced, what would happen the next day. You told of spending free time reading current best sellers, teaching yourself about the stock market, and making investments in a few stocks as a way to jump-start our future. You also wrote about your memories of me, your hopes for our life together when you returned, and always your love. I adored the "ja elska da" that you used in closing so many of those letters. It meant so much to me just to see your script, where I found myself becoming aware of slight differences in intensity and slant and then trying to guess what you must have felt like on that particular day. I reread every word, every page, hundreds of times. Your letters became the most important part of my daily life. I must admit as I reread them now, I see concerns of yours that I don't recall having noticed in those initial readings—concerns that foreshadowed some of our more difficult times. How could you have known those things? Why didn't I?

I returned to my own "tour of duty" at summer camp, when school got out in June. I began to realize through my teaching that spring and in my art work that summer that I had found my mission. Troubled teens found a new, safe way to express themselves through projects that I devised for them. This feeling of having an impact helped to compensate for the emotional support that was lacking in my camp counselor peers.

"So, Cathy, what the hell is wrong with that guy of yours, John whoever-he-is?" Dan said to me the first night at camp after our orientation session. "Nobody who's anybody enlists, unless he's a John Bircher or something. Don't tell me you've fallen for one of those guys!"

"His decision had nothing to *do* with politics," I'd respond.

"Yeah, Cath, really. You might want to think this thing over, I mean about getting married and everything," Jane suggested. "There are other guys, you know, guys who believe in peace. Doesn't that make more sense, I mean to marry someone who believes in the things you do?"

"As if she could possibly understand," I'd think to myself, and then try to explain, "It's not like he wanted to go to war. He had no choice, really."

"He had no choice?" questioned Steve. "What are you talking about? He could've gone to Canada! I know lots of guys from my high school who went to Toronto. It's great up there. The war will be over soon, and then they'll be back—with both legs, I might add!"

"That really makes me feel better," I'd say under my breath, adding with a bit of sarcasm and a louder voice, "That's a great idea, Steve. I'll suggest that one to John in my next letter. I am sure it never occurred to him!" I knew that they were absolutely incapable of comprehending your decision, so I stopped talking about you. To say that the war was unpopular is a bit of an understatement. I knew that you really had no choice after losing your student status. Those without the forced choice were clueless and more than a bit judgmental.

Summer camp, our plan to meet in Hawaii during your Christmas leave, and the distractions of my last semester at the University filled my days and helped me persevere. I made space in my life every day to write about everything going on in my world and inside my head. I get the impression as I reread your letters that I may have complained a bit too much. You spoke often about wanting to make me happy, about my needing to make the most out of my circumstances, of the importance of enjoying the summer evenings and fall foliage. I didn't mean to complain or to suggest that my loneliness was greater than yours. I guess I wanted you to know that I understood your loneliness, and mine made me feel just that much closer to you. I must have written to you about my dreams for a home and family with you someday, for you also wrote about our need to be patient with those kinds of goals, that we would have them one day but not all at once. I think perhaps my needs worried you. Is that what it was? I didn't mean for my thoughts to produce that effect. Of course, we would have to wait for a house and children and many more things, too. I never minded the idea of waiting, as long as I waited with you. I thought that it was a good idea to talk about these things at some point.

The Winter and Spring of 1968

The New Year's week together in Hawaii during your leave was probably our finest ever. From that first moment when my eyes found yours in the hotel lobby to our last embrace at the airport amidst the tropical flowers, the palm trees, the setting sun, and loving tears, we were truly in paradise. You were so thoughtful to plan that week—the timing of it, more specifically—accommodating both my final exam schedule and my parents' wish to have me home for Christmas. To the present moment as I write this letter, I recall those seven days and am drawn right back to the passion I experienced and to the person whom I knew I could not live without. Saying good-bye in Honolulu and wishing for the days to pass until the wedding—neither of us could imagine that we would ever have to endure such insurmountable agony again. Nothing could be worse, we imagined. We were young, of course, naive and inexperienced in the way life weaves its story.

We initially planned a summer wedding. We opted for April when the Army approved your request for an earlier release, thus making it possible for you to return to school in September. Your assignment: a base in Texas and five more months apart—unless we could get married first! You wrote my parents a letter asking for their permission to move the wedding date up two months, realizing that there was no other way for us to be together. Neither of us could fathom extending our separation for that impossible length of time! This is another of those life events that seems so foolish in retrospect, surely an item for an "overs" list of things that I would have done differently if given the chance again. Once I knew that you were coming home sooner rather than later, I desperately insisted to my parents that the wedding had to be sooner as well. I can see now that a later date (even with the added suffering) or perhaps an elopement in Hawaii, would have been better for all of us. There was so much stress, such anxiety associated with planning the wedding under those time pressures. It was supposed to be such a happy time, just as it had been for Liz; but it was nothing of the kind. As hard as it was for me, it was even harder for you.

I began to have second thoughts about our decision the minute I saw you getting off the plane at the Milwaukee airport, after a year of service in Vietnam. The wedding was just days away. Both families were already gathering at my home for the pre-wedding celebrations. You searched the crowd and upon finding my face, smiled and came straight toward me with arms open wide for the embrace that I'd waited so long to receive, the one saying "hello" forever and no more sad good-byes. Within moments and before leaving the airport, you indicated that you needed to excuse yourself before becoming terribly ill. We were both so happy, yet so unraveled. I realized that you felt the stress of it all far more than I did, having been literally half a world away for so long. Your last letters from Vietnam revealed a greater level of anxiety and fear as the war efforts escalated during the Tet Offensive of '68. You were never involved in combat, yet experienced a degree of trauma nonetheless. It really wasn't wise for either of us, but especially not for you, to push things so fast. Our parents said as much; but we were not about to listen, not after what we had been through. We prevailed. We wanted that wedding, and we wanted it then! Maybe because most of our friends were getting married at the same time, it just seemed like the right thing to do.

We needed more time, John—time for you to decompress, time to renew our relationship, time to get to know one another again and in person. So much had happened in both of our lives, and there was no chance to bring each other up to date. It could be that we imagined our letters were accomplishing that task, another sign of our naivete. We had been together for exactly two months total between January of 1966 (when we last broke up) and our wedding in April of

1968. Two months out of nearly two and a half years! We were better pen pals than partners initially. What were we thinking? Do you remember showing slides of Southeast Asia to my parents and grandmother in our living room just 36 hours after leaving Vietnam? How bizarre was that!

I noticed that you were at least 40 pounds lighter, had a definite nervousness in your voice, a tremor in your hands, all of which made me concerned for your well-being. I was somewhat worried as well about your increased need for cigarettes and alcohol, but I never said anything. Everyone is nervous before a wedding. Furthermore, I knew that everyone drank in Vietnam and that many used marijuana to relieve the stress. Your need for alcohol was more than I had remembered, and perhaps I expected it to diminish in time. While in Vietnam or after returning home, you never wrote or spoke about witnessing terrible events or feeling great terror—experiences that would explain, maybe even justify, your drinking so much. To the contrary, you recalled your year of service as downright boring most of the time, with the exception of the last month or so. I mention this now because I've racked my brain trying to find a "start date" and maybe then to discover a cause for your addiction. I am so confused. I can't think about it anymore. I only know that I found it so much easier to focus on the wedding. If there were problems, we could deal with them later.

You seemed to think that I was a beautiful bride. I know that I radiated with happiness and pride as I contemplated our new life together. Even our honeymoon car trip around Wisconsin, visiting friends and relatives, was wonderful. I look back on that time and realize now that I probably would do it all over again. I saw what I wanted to see, my handsome soldier in full-dress uniform. It seemed so perfect. I wanted it to be so perfect. It wasn't so perfect after all, but it took us many years to realize that truth.

Love,

Cathy

Ft. Leonard Wood, Mo.
December 5, 1966

Dear Cathy,

12 days and counting. Can't wait!

. . . A guy from the University of Kansas and I took our passes together. We didn't go any place Fri. Night—just slept and would have liked to stay in bed Sat. also. But passes—like everything else in the army—have strings attached.

Sat. Morning we had to get out of the barracks by 5:30 A.M. or we would have been put on details like everyone else—so immediately after breakfast we walked to the bus station and stood in zero weather 1½ hours waiting for them to open. I still don't know if that beat details. But anyway at 8 A.M. we caught a bus to Columbia, 100 miles north, and the home of Missouri University. You have no idea how great it was to ride down the highway and see billboards, houses, Xmas decorations, and towns. Was like getting out of jail—whatever that's like. . . .

We got to Columbia at noon and being true G.I.'s went to the first bar we saw. I started on Martinis and after that have only scattered memories. They aren't clear at all. Jim, my accomplice, says I slapped a lot of backs like I'd known people a long time—unfortunately I don't remember that. I do remember walking into a bar at 7:15 but leaving immediately because I thought it was 1 A.M. and closing time. We went bowling sometime after dark . . . . Jim fell down on the alley and I threw my ball backwards twice. . . .

We're counting the days and I can't wait. . . . I have no idea when I'll get home again after Xmas so I hope I can be with you all the time.

Send my love,

John

Vietnam Air Force Base
April 13, 1967

Dear Cathy,

It seems strange to be writing to you from the other side of the world. It's 8 A.M. Thurs. here in V.N., but in Milwaukee it's 6 P.M. Wed. Really a weird feeling. I just finished breakfast and you are probably just sitting down to yesterday's dinner. Hard to comprehend-the time difference is 14 hrs. ahead of CST-so when you get up in the morning, you can think of me just going to bed. . . .

. . . Cam Rand Bay is quite an area. It made a beautiful picture from the air-dark blue sea with many bays-all with huge white sand beaches-and in the background deep green hills-and mountains. . . . It's almost like a resort-There are movies every night on an outdoor screen, and everyone simply lies in the sand to watch the picture. . . A no-car drive-in. This is a very secure area-with any danger of V.C. virtually impossible, so the only way we know that we are in V.N. is by the heat. And it is hot, just like the hottest, most humid day of August in Wisc. . . Still have no idea of where I'm going. . .

. . . I don't think it is necessary to discuss my dating girls. It seems pretty silly—even if I had a chance over here—you know I wouldn't. As far as what you do—I don't expect you to sit at home every night—but I trust your judgment—without any doubt. And anything you do is fine with me. I think we can trust each other enough to not worry about things like that. The thing I worry about, and the only thing, is your happiness, and I know you have to stay busy doing things to be happy, so stay busy. Just remember, I love you more than anything (and I mean anything) in the world.

I think of you always—Love,

John

Vietnam

Sunday [End of January, 1968]

Dear Mom + Dad-

Hawaii was beautiful. I'm afraid it's pretty hard to start writing letters again from Pleihu after being with Cathy and in civilization for a week. . . . I'm hoping we'll be busier than ever at the office so I can keep my mind off my homesickness - But I'll be home in 86 days at the longest so it shouldn't be too bad. . . .Hawaii really was fantastic. The island is beautiful-all the palm trees. . . the pineapple fields. . . .But everything we saw and did was sort of like a roving violinist playing background music, because the all important thing was being with Cathy-We are really very deeply in love, and it's such a most beautiful feeling-am getting anxious for the wedding day.

Will write again soon
Love

John

Vietnam
Feb. 16, 1968

Dear Cathy-

Hi there-for the moment we are caught up on work so I have a break to write!. . . . a new first. I have been going to the movies lately. . . am in the middle of reading The Source which is very enjoyable. . . . and that is the extent of my social life. Tonight I shall spend a fun-packed evening on guard-We have a full moon these days (I imagine you have the same moon!) lots of stars and I shall spend the entire evening dreaming of you, my love- . . . I did tell you to polish your riding boots, didn't I? You see I'm still planning on the April wedding . . . I love you a bunch.-till tomorrow-

John

CHAPTER 3

EARLY YEARS OF MARRIAGE

Alcohol Dependency Grows

April 30, 1997

Dear John,

TEXAS, 1968

I wonder if those first years of marriage would have been different if someone had told me what to expect. I was like so many of my friends in that regard. We all must have lived out our youth with the same "Ozzie and Harriet" mythology drifting through our minds. We'd be loving and polite and have well-mannered children. I imagined romantic dinners, complete with candles and wine, sweet little apartments with matching curtains and table cloths. You'd leave for work each morning, kissing me good-bye, missing me terribly all day long, then come home to greet me with a bouquet of roses, and we'd always have enough money to spend.

Maybe the fiction explains why I felt such a sense of disappointment when we drove into the blazing heat of Texas in April of 1968. That day still flashes before my eyes with all the clarity and aroma of this morning's cup of coffee, minus any soothing effect. Little did we know that in order for you to return to the UW in September to complete your undergraduate degree, we first had to survive Duncanville Nike Missile Base. No "newly-wed" status for us!

"Get out of the car, SOLDIER!" an officer of some rank shouted to you as we pulled forward past the entrance gate.

"You stay here, Cath. I'll handle this," you said to me out of the officer's earshot. You told me later that you were not allowed to speak in these circumstances.

"So what have we HERE?" he demanded, walking to within an inch of your chest. "A slimy, son-of-a-bitch

SOLDIER who doesn't remember what a UNIFORM is! Where's your HAT, soldier? Don't you underSTAND that you are under orders FROM the United States government to dress AT ALL TIMES in full UNIFORM?" he blasted in a voice that must have been audible in the next county, and with his face tomato red and eyes fully bulging from beneath a visored cap. "Is that too complicated for you to REMEMBER? ANSWER ME, SOLDIER, OR DID YOU LOSE YOUR HEARING, TOO?"

"Sir, I'm sorry, Sir. I lost my hat in Nam, Sir," you answered with eyes staring through him somehow so as not to be accused of gazing inappropriately.

"Oh, so you've been in Nam," he said with an unfelt look of sympathy as he clasped his hands behind his back and repositioned his legs in a broader stance. "Do you think that MAKES YOU SPECIAL? Get your ass out of my face before I puke!" Finally, the officer turned to leave but pivoted back for one last shot: "If you don't get a hat in the next 10 minutes, you'll wish you were back in Nam, Soldier. DID YOU HEAR ME? I'M TALKING TO YOU!"

My bubble burst at that very instant. I don't remember your being shocked by this treatment, this total lack of respect, this display of power, and the pleasure your superior exhibited in humiliating you in front of me. Maybe you grew accustomed to it after all of those months of training and service. I certainly was not and was absolutely stunned. I immediately wanted to defend you, to protect you. I wanted to tell that officer about the level of responsibility that you shouldered in Vietnam and of the respect that you earned from all who served with you. I lost my Midwest naivete in that moment, but you had already lost yours.

I always wondered why we never really talked about the war. Possibly you figured that your experiences were ones that I could never fully comprehend. I knew that your assignment in the accounting office was relatively safe and that you never experienced combat. You were far away from home, and that was enough trauma for all of us. I suppose that you may have wanted to forget it all, at least the stressful parts, and to continue with life from where we left off. That does make sense. It just doesn't work, especially when we didn't even have a solid leaving-off place to which we could return. I was so proud of you. I thought I could heal any remaining wounds by being a devoted, loving wife.

Weren't those first months of our marriage—the "Texas Trial" I like to call it now—a true reality check if there ever was one? Our tiny upstairs apartment, the surgery to remove that terrible cyst in my neck, your unending paperwork for unknown purposes, and my job as a clerk at J.C. Penney's. Remember?

"Hi, Shugga," a cowboy would saunter up to me and say. "Where y'all keep yer tee vees?"

"The television department is straight ahead, just past the lamps on your right-hand side," I'd explain, unknowingly revealing my origins.

"Oh, Ah see. Yer a nawthin'er. Ah knew y'all weren't from araun' these parts. But yer maghty pritty anyways, Ah say." He'd tip his well-worn, western-style hat toward me and then be on his way. Soon I'd be approached by someone else, perhaps an older woman in town for the day.

"Dawlin', kin you help me?" she'd ask.

" What country did I land in," I wondered to myself, "where no one would ever call me 'Miss' or 'Ma'am,' much less by my given name?"

"Ah jus' mus' find some a' dem draws," she'd explain.

"Oh, certainly, Ma'am." I'd answer confidently. "The furniture department is on Two. You can take the elevator."

"Whut AH you tawkin' 'bout? AH di'n't say 'draws.' Ah said 'DRAWS'" she'd repeat, making a distinct effort to enunciate more clearly.

"I am so sorry." I'd say apologetically. "It must be the fan that's keeping me from hearing you properly. Of course, intimate apparel is right behind us and to the left." "How do these people understand each other?" I asked myself. I truly felt that one of us must be speaking a foreign language. I got used to it, though, and actually found myself picking up a bit of an accent after a while.

We did love the horseback riding, and you—the cards and vodka with your sergeant and his wife. I remember your weaving home one night and getting the first of many citations for Driving While Intoxicated (a DWI). I remember, too, how you were able to get out of it by making up some story, the first of a long line of successful performances, convincing the police that a ticket or fine was just not called for in your particular situation. You clearly had a gift for persuasion, a skill that served you well in your later lobbying years. Thankfully, we weren't in Texas long.

Madison

Wisconsin never looked so good to me as it did after that unyielding, dusty-hot summer. I think back now and realize how fortunate we were during those few lean years that followed that I was always able to come up with teaching positions each time we moved. My small income carried us through. Moreover, I loved teaching, due in part both to my students and to the new friends we made. Carol and Kenyon, Cam and Noreen: Both couples became regular players in our lives as colleagues as well as for weekend social activities. You and Kenyon became especially close after discovering common interests ranging from politics and finance to late-night conversations with a bottle of brandy.

We all drank more than we should have in those days, myself included. It was different, though, for the women. Carol and I could sip for hours on a single glass of wine—perhaps two— bonding more through conversation. You and Kenyon typically downed five or six drinks, probably even more when the evening began with an early dinner. I remember one night, in particular, when we all nearly got kicked out of "The Springs" dining room. We all thought it was so funny at the time, our raucous behavior in the famed Frank Lloyd Wright restaurant near the small rural town of Spring Green. We determined—in our somewhat arrogant, inebriated states—that these country folk just couldn't relate to us sophisticated urban dwellers. To be honest, our behavior probably was rather outrageous. I seem to remember myself drinking most of the time, though, just to be a part of the group. Really, there is no way to feel more like a "fifth wheel" than to be the only sober person at the party, or so it appeared to me.

The simple truth is that we all got into a pattern of drinking to excess. I really don't know why we did.

We seemed to be having a good time—laughing at jokes, telling stories, making critical comments about other patrons; but then with you, it always got out of hand. It wasn't just once in a while either. It was many nights of brandy and cigarettes and laughing and jokes and games and close calls driving home. Maybe that's where it all got started for you. I know you drank well before that in high school, in college, and in Vietnam. But the really serious drinking with the hard liquor, that was new to me. First in Texas, then in Madison, and then in every other place that we lived: Alcohol became a permanent fixture. We were with people, of course, who made it seem like the thing to do.

I have wondered when drinking first became a regular part of your daily life. Was it in college or before? Or was it after? I must have made it easy for you, for all of us. I never objected to it. I actually enjoyed it sometimes. That was how the evenings were spent in my home when I was growing up and again when I returned while completing my student teaching as a senior in college. To me, what we were doing—you and I, that is—seemed so normal, so "adult." I also have wondered why *I* didn't become the alcoholic. It was my family, after all, that had the history, not yours. Drinking seemed to make me tired, but it transformed you into a totally different person. While sober, you appeared shy and uncomfortable, withdrawn and serious. After a few drinks, you'd loosen up and become the life of the party. You made people laugh, made others feel that you were their best friend. Maybe you just liked the freedom it fostered. I don't have an answer, of course, just a few speculations.

CHICAGO, 1970

When you graduated from the University in 1970 (earning a 4.00 for 4 straight semesters, I might add!) and took that first position as a purchasing agent with Allied Van Lines in Chicago, Carol and Kenyon were replaced by another partying couple. To me, it was still such fun—those wild nights in Greek Town and the 48-hour weekend blitzes, putting away more than a few bottles of cheap wine with our new friends. I loved my Chicago teaching, the family get-togethers there with your sister, Clarice, and her husband, Jim. I realize now, when I think back, that we really enjoyed seeing them and your darling niece, Kim. Whatever happened to those relationships? We rarely saw them in later years, and we never really thought about why we let that happen. Did our drinking push them away or offend them somehow? Or did we become so self-absorbed in our own life after our children were born that we never paid them any attention? The two of us had few talks of any serious nature about these or any other kinds of matters, but we did know how to have fun. Chicago was good to us; but we enjoyed ourselves even more by getting out of the city and into the country, where you especially felt more at ease. That is where we began our hobby of hunting for unusual antiques at quaint farm auctions.

The time in Chicago was short; and within less than a year, thanks to Kenyon's maneuvering, we were back in Madison. I don't recall all of the details, but somehow he helped you secure a position with the Wisconsin Department of Revenue. You left your job in Chicago in March to begin the new one, while I stayed to finish out the spring school term. To keep me company, my grandmother paid a visit. No one could bring a smile to my face faster than Gramma Torrison.

"Tell me honestly, my darling Catherine, isn't the Seurat the most magnificent work at the Institute?" she'd ask with a Hermione Gingold lilt in her voice.

Or, "We simply MUST go to Saks this instant," she'd announce while sipping her coffee, eating her scone, and listing her errands on a clean piece of stationery. "They're having a fashion show for cruise wear—not that I can see myself spending an entire WEEK with a parade of people whom I've never met. It's just important—imperative, really—to keep abreast of the latest trends."

Or before bed, "Catherine, Catherine, Catherine. I absolutely believe you have the most exquisite—no, the most divine—taste in upholstery. That fabric is stunning! I'm quite sure if we get down to Fields tomorrow, we'll find the perfect pillow to complete the concept."

There were no serious conversations, of course. With Gramma, that was next to impossible. The only mildly serious moment I can recall during that visit was her "negotiating" with the maître d' at the famed Lilac Lounge for a center table in the Safari Room. I never asked about Grandpa Torrison or his problems with alcohol, because it would be years before I fully understood the nature of his fatal illness. Nor did I ask Gramma about her leaving him, when his drinking became more than she could manage. Not many women had the courage in those days to face the world as a single parent, much less to go to work to support her children when most of her peers were preparing for tea parties. We did keep a lot of secrets, we Turmos and Torrisons. I know we were good at it and still are, as a matter of fact.

During the separation that spring, John, there were no lonely love letters and few phone calls from you, just occasional weekends together when the weather permitted me to drive to Wisconsin.

Madison, 1971

Meanwhile, your new position rewarded you well and matched your talents perfectly. I was so excited to be a part of it all, meeting people in the Governor's office and being invited to social engagements. Our lives slowly separated, however. The Wagon Wheel, a bar near the state office building, became an after-hours "office" for the requisite schmoozing with all of the "big boys," a responsibility that you claimed "came with the territory." While you worked that summer, I began transforming our Cape Cod starter home on Eton Ridge into a showplace. You did the carpentry and electrical work on weekends, trusting me to make all decorating decisions. I wallpapered the bedrooms, rosemaled the kitchen cupboards, stripped and varnished the hardwood floors, and hung my original and collected works of art. This was our very first home, and I wanted to live there forever!

When fall came, I again found myself completely involved in teaching—first in Mt. Horeb and then in Madison—all the while continuing my own painting at home, my "little art stuff" as you generally referred to it. I'll have to admit that we'd have had little bread on the table were we solely dependent upon my painting, even during the very best years of art fairs and the occasional gallery. Maybe that's what you meant by that comment of yours, which did bother me. It bothered me, in fact, until I reread your letters recently. It is a mystery to me that I never actually noticed how often you wrote about my work. You asked me so many times to send photos of paintings as I completed them so that you could show them to the guys and have something from me to decorate your barracks. You spoke of comments that others there would make about my talent and how lucky you were. For some reason, I repressed those comments. Who knows why? Anyway, whatever artistic flare I developed, it most definitely is what helps my business now. No, gift baskets aren't paintings; but let me tell you, John, they *are* putting a little bread on the table. I am very proud of that—but I am getting side-tracked here.

There was another time during those first pre-children years that I wonder if you remember. It was our fourth Christmas together in 1972, the time we went to Florida. If you don't remember, I am not surprised, as nothing really remarkable happened. I remember it vividly for two unrelated reasons. First, it was the only Christmas that we did not spend in Wisconsin before or after the children were born. All others throughout our entire marriage were spent on the highway traveling completely across the state between Viroqua and Wauwatosa so that we could share that most important of holidays with both of our families. Neither of us ever looked forward to the trek, which occasionally meant fighting a raging snow storm and most certainly, icy roads. It felt so good in that single instance to be in one place for a change and to have some reprieve from the arctic cold that most definitely hovered over Wisconsin by late

December. Never mind that the experience in Florida was not especially pleasurable.

Now where was I? Oh, yes, there was a second reason for my remembering our Florida Christmas. We arrived exhausted after the 28-hour drive and got a nice hotel in the coastal village of Vero Beach, just off the beach itself. We'd go out to dinner, have a "few" drinks, go back to the hotel, and soon you would fall asleep from too much alcohol, I presumed. We met two fun-loving couples from Canada. You might recall that part. Then it was the six of us eating, having our drinks, and talking loudly at the pool the next day. More significantly, this was the time when I began to feel uncomfortable with your drinking. I wondered whether my annoying tachycardia were linked to my own drinking behavior. I recall sensing that alcohol was becoming a problem for both of us. I believed that I would have no difficulty cutting down on my consumption of alcohol, if that were necessary; and a subsequent check-up when we returned indicated that it was. I feared that you might find abstinence—or even drinking in a more controlled manner—impossible, and I was right. For some reason, you needed it to get through each and every day. And you had built up such a tolerance level that one or two drinks were simply not enough.

I recall a few other times later that spring when your alcohol consumption was way out of control, so much so that it became an embarrassment to me. You were still with the Department of Revenue, I think; and your boss, Bob, brought you home one evening after "work" totally inebriated. The two of you obviously had been out together; but, John, this was your boss we are talking about, not just a colleague. I had never met the man before, and there I was alone with him in our living room, not knowing what to say. I felt so humiliated. I didn't know what to offer as an excuse for your behavior, or if it would be better for me to distract him by talking about something completely unrelated. Of course, that's what I did. And there was another time shortly after that when Karen, a teacher friend of mine, asked me about your drinking after seeing you fall into the radiator at our home. I also became increasingly uncomfortable with those Saturday afternoons of treasure hunting at rural auctions. Oh, they started out wonderfully and enabled us to furnish our entire home in a truly eclectic manner for a fraction of the cost of store-bought items. Those adventures, however, always ended up in some country tavern where you got drunk, carrying on with perfect strangers whom we'd never see again. I drank to dull my senses at times but was uncomfortable, embarrassed, and apprehensive. During this entire time, I never got the feeling that you felt the least bit concerned. I have no excuse for never talking with you about it. I am completely clueless as to why I chose not even to bring it up.

Even worse, I don't have an excuse for my part in our drinking with another couple whom we met in our church's Bible study group—and right in front of the minister! What were we thinking? Did the alcohol convince us that no one else knew we had been drinking? Our minister was one of the few people to confront you, John. We have to acknowledge that. He tried to reach out to us, to warn us both, to help us. We did not reach back. We were far from even admitting that we had a problem and even less ready to listen to any advice. The concern that I first felt in

Florida and the embarrassment that I experienced at home were not strong enough for me to change my own behavior, much less to confront you about yours. There's a tremendous distance between insight and action, especially when insight is so short-lived.

I reread these next letters of yours a few days ago. I remember Susie's wedding, in particular, as if it were yesterday—my orange bride's maid gown, her dress of ivory, and that beautiful summer day. I was so happy for her and for Jacque, but at the same time I felt so sad for us. Why couldn't it be our wedding day? Now I am asking a different question: Why did I lay all of these thoughts on you?

Love,

Cath

Vietnam
June 3, 1967

Dear Cathy,

. . . So guess what I did yesterday—my afternoon off—2 long showers—one before my 3-hour nap and one after—not the most exciting but sure felt good. I felt so good that Jack and I went to the club last night and had a few drinks—and really had a very good time talking about everything. I even went over my budget spending $1.30, which opened everyone's eyes—since I've sort of gotten the rep. of a tight wad by sticking to $1.00 a day budget, which includes everything from soda to film (I've given up soda because it's .20 per). . . . But it's worth it since the nest egg is very slowly growing and will soon be safely in stock. . . Think of you always.

Love,

John

Vietnam
June 12, 1967

Dear Cathy,

. . . I was glad to get all your letters written during the wedding. Your mood sounded much like the one I was in while writing my last few letters to you. I can only guess what caused your moods—but I can try—and certainly understand a whole year is an awfully long time and letters—a very poor substitute for being close, especially in those moments when it is really important to have one person close. To say the least, it is very difficult. And believe me, when I write letters full of depression and the hardship we have here—what is really the underlying cause is knowing that you, although not isolated, are alone. And I also know that you are carrying the brunt of the hardship by not only being alone but also having to be with people—people whom we both know and probably even harder—people whom you know alone and have to answer their questions about my being in V.N. and about our far-from-gold-plated immediate future—and I'm very sorry—and get depressed when I think about it—But I also know that I love you more that anything in the world and want nothing but to make your life a part of mine—and that you love me in return and that ultimately is the only lasting and important thing. But we have to recognize the difficulties we have—and pray earnestly for strength.

I wish the days away.

My love,

John

Vietnam
July 1, 1967

Dear Cathy,

. . . Quote of the day from Mia Farrow in _Life_, May 29—". . . the world is what you make of it: Who says it has to be four walls, three windows and a rug on the floor? That's called convention—good for the masses and for the order of things—but I don't want it written on my tombstone." Of course, you realize that I'm not saying we're going to live in a tepee on a pile of dreams—but just that my desires in life go a lot farther than being satisfied with trying to make payments on a house . . . in the suburbs. There are too many great things in the world to do—to allow yourself to get caught up in the "convention," conventional way of doing them. The house in the suburbs is a necessity—but the approach to it is the problem—Too many people look on the house and everything it stands for, as the ultimate goal in life—and in effect—the end of life—and the whole idea is stifling in itself. . . . . . . But no need to ramble on about that because I know you agree-And everything I want from life-has you standing right beside me-forever -

I love you always.

John

An Khe Vietnam
July 23, 1967

Dear Cath –

It finally happened. . . . We had a real whopper of a Bourbon spree last night. All started quite innocently with all of us going to the club for our nightly 2 beers. . . But then the manager of the club. . . broke out a quart of bourbon . . . . Wow–Definitely a whopper. . . . Was a real battle pulling my mangled body out of bed. . But now at the ungodly hour of 9 I feel great again. . . mainly because I just received 2 letters from you. Although I must admit being a little upset with you for feeling stifled at camp and wanting to see someone from the "outside"– even tho I understand very well what you mean because that is exactly my situation here–except when I read it from you, I compare my state with yours and get upset because I want you to make the most of the lake, the horses, and even Sat. Eves in the bar. Like I said I understand what you feel and why . . . but think that perhaps that feeling is unwarranted.

But I shant go into a sob story about isolation . . .

Ja elska da

John

CHAPTER 4

MARRIAGE AND FAMILY

Denial, Deceit, and Destruction

May 16, 1997

Dear John,

The last letter took a lot out of me, which is why it has taken me so long to get back to writing again about the children. I am beginning to see myself in a different light now. Somehow over the years, I always managed to discount your behaviors in a conversation with myself. "John must have a lot on his mind," or "I can't believe what that boss of John's is expecting him to do, just to get a bill through the Legislature!" or "He's never been this far gone, this completely unconscious. I know he won't want this ever to happen again. He could die!" It was easier to rationalize, to blame someone else, or to convince myself that you would eventually want to give up drinking yourself—easier than it was to face the truth and contend with the crisis that I was convinced would follow. I really never saw anyone in your condition before. Even within my family, I was shielded carefully from all of the ugliness, only managing to pry details loose from relatives decades later. A lot of good that did! But let me leave those times for now and talk about the children.

Still in Madison, 1973

Our lives changed a great deal over the course of the next several years. In January of 1973, your father passed away. No other individual would ever take his place as the most influential person in your life—your conscience, to some extent—and your grief was shared by all who knew him. Out of the emptiness and the despair that followed, we decided to try to begin a family of our own. We were so excited later that fall to learn that I was finally pregnant. Perhaps due to all of our stress, I had almost given up hope that I would ever conceive; but we were truly blessed. You were so proud when you called your mother to tell her that we were expecting and were absolutely thrilled—I can still see the relief on your face—when Kristin made her entry into the world in May of 1974. From that very first day, she was your little princess. What you would have given for your father to have had the chance to hold her in his arms!

John, it meant so much to me to have you there for that first labor and delivery. Maybe I didn't tell you how much I needed you and how grateful I was that fathers-to-be were finally allowed in the delivery room. I never got over your being out of town when Nels was born exactly one year later and my having to go through it all alone. I felt deserted and scared, hurt and embarrassed. Husbands are supposed to be there at those times. Expectant fathers just don't let business deals cause them to miss the births of their children, I reasoned. Certainly no father who missed the birth of his first son would have the nerve to arrive at the hospital the next day visibly drunk. But you did! I believe that it was then, while in the hospital with our first son and our one-year-old daughter at home, that I felt us losing our foothold. I chose to focus my attention not on our marriage but on the children. I didn't really think that I had another choice.

Those first years of parenthood were so chaotic. Kristin gave us such a scare with her breathing problems and seizures. Thank heavens she was ultimately okay, but for months we did not know if she would grow up to be healthy and normal. Meanwhile, you jumped from one business venture to the next, certain that each one would lead to instant wealth.

First there was the land development scheme with your older cousin, who expected you to live on savings until there was a profit to share. Naturally, there were no profits that came our way. Meanwhile all of your traveling and marketing and entertaining expenses totally drained our small reserves, while forcing us to live on credit. When your cousin announced that the project failed, he did not offer you any compensation. Instead, he came back to you with a plan to sell cattle to Costa Rica. We got out of it all when our debt hit $40,000. Really, John, those were pretty ridiculous chances to take when we had nothing to fall back on and were just starting our family. I was as relieved as you when you were offered a position in Milwaukee, even if it meant leaving the house we had completely remodeled and absolutely loved. There were two little mouths to feed at the time and a third child on the way. We needed a solid, steady income. We needed even more to get out of debt as the stress of it began to affect our marriage. We were thankful that my father's loan prevented us from going into complete bankruptcy.

MILWAUKEE, 1977

We started over in Milwaukee for the fifth time in five years. We believed a change of venue would allow us to wipe the slate clean again, giving us a chance for a new beginning. I remember so clearly the day we walked into our new home for the first time, right after finishing the paperwork for our loan at the bank. You stopped me in the entrance way, turned me toward you and said, "I know that we almost lost it all, Cath, but more important than anything, I realize now that I almost lost you." Then you held me in your arms, feeling the little one inside me kicking and turning. You kissed me, and I just knew this would be a wonderful new chapter in our lives. I replay moments like that one over and over in my mind, reassuring myself that you did love me—once upon a time—and that you wanted the "happily ever after" as much as did I.

I think back on those days and realize now that the idea of having a family was more my idea than yours. I assumed you would want children, but having them so fast was not part of our plan. I know they brought joy to your life in many ways, but perhaps the timing was not right for you. You felt such pressure from both of our families to be successful, and the pressure grew when our own family grew. I am sure that my father's attitude only worsened the situation. He never approved of our marriage, never thought you would provide well enough for me, never forgave our need to ask him for money; and you must have sensed that attitude whenever he was present with all of his huffing around. I probably added to the burden. I did love the big Lincoln Continental that your cousin got for you when you two were partners, the regular social engagements that gave me a chance to dress "to the nines," the "power people" in your life whom I got to meet, our Tudor-style Milwaukee home with leaded windows, 12-foot ceilings, hardwood floors, and a gracious sun room—perhaps more than we really could afford at the time. I convinced myself that this was what you wanted, too. Perhaps I should have reread that "Mia Farrow" reference in your letter again.

Something began to grate on me more and more though, John, after that move. I'm sure it was a constellation of factors that produced my own high-stress condition. Those were difficult times on virtually every dimension, no question about it. My father died of cancer a few weeks after we moved into our new home. Lars was born exactly four weeks after that (with you barely making it to the hospital in time). And then, of course, there was my newly-widowed mother with her own, complex health problems. Why her dilemmas all fell on my shoulders to manage and became my responsibility to resolve, I don't really know. I only know that there seemed to be no choice in the matter, given that my brother and sister moved to the west coast many years earlier and, thus, were in no reasonable proximity to help. Taking care of three small children—the oldest one not even being three years of age—left not a single moment of time for myself—not for my painting, for a bath, or even for a cup of coffee. It was coughs and croupe, diapers and laundry, feedings and toys, too many tears and too few naps! I know that I was more than a little frazzled with the entire weight of it all.

Whatever the reason, I grew less and less tolerant of your embarrassing binges, almost all of them occurring during social engagements with important power people on whom you thrived. Do you remember when a colleague of yours and his fiancée arranged to take us to a baseball game with box-seat tickets? I knew your colleague (I think his name was John), but never had met his fiancée before they arrived at our doorstep. I found myself having to entertain them both alone, until you arrived, late as usual and so drunk that you could not speak. I noticed the two of them exchanging concerned glances, not knowing how to relieve my embarrassment. Then there were the fund-raising events where your drinking made you totally incoherent, the evenings when you came in late and just passed out on the couch, and other nights when without any warning you never came home at all. We had no relationship, no marriage to speak of for those two years that we lived in Milwaukee. We used the same address to receive our mail, but there were no family dinners or breakfasts together. The children were in bed on those few occasions when you did come home. I worried that they might never know their father. I felt like I was living a nightmare.

I didn't know where to turn for help but hoped that one of those marriage encounters announced in church one Sunday might be the answer for us.

"You want us to do what?" you asked, with a look that seemed to imply that I was absolutely nuts. "Yeah, right. I can just see it. Some psychologist with his simplistic program is going to tell me to get in touch with my inner self, and then poof! You and I are going to ride off into the sunset, happily ever after." And then for added emphasis, you laughed your way to the liquor cabinet.

"Well, John, then you figure this out. All I know is that we don't have a life any more, and here is something that might help. How do we know it won't work until we try?" I asked. "It's free, you know. Maybe we'll meet some new people."

"Like I really need to meet some new people. That's what John needs: some NEW PEOPLE, some CHURCH PEOPLE, some people who KNOW JESUS. Okay, Catherine, if it would make you happy," you said with your usual tinge of sarcasm and after pouring yourself another drink, "but don't say I didn't warn you. It'll make about as big a difference as doing a rain dance in the desert."

I knew you would think it was ridiculous; but if you remember, your drinking did taper off a bit, at least initially. Within weeks of the encounter, however, you resumed your all-too-familiar behaviors; but now the timing quadrupled the impact.

It was Christmas Eve. You left the house to see a neighbor for what was supposed to be a short chat. I washed the dishes, read the children a Christmas Eve favorite of mine, "'Twas the Night before Christmas," and then after putting them to bed, went downstairs to make a pot of coffee. I knew we'd be up late wrapping packages, as was our tradition, and I gathered up all the gifts from their hiding places around the house. I waited and waited and finished my coffee before finally realizing that you were not coming home. I went ahead wrapping gifts alone, guessing that you were drinking again. I considered phoning you as two hours became four; but by that time, I was already too hurt and too angry to care. You finally returned in the wee hours of the morning, barely able to walk through the front door. You promptly proceeded to pass out in the living room on the couch, never coming out of it through the entire Christmas Day. The kids opened their gifts and played as you slept it off, snoring in the background. They were so young, perhaps too young to realize that this was not the way it was supposed to be. My mother was not too old, however, to see the picture for what it really was. Luckily, a couple of drinks kept her from bothering me with questions or comments.

You knew that I was upset when you finally did wake up. I knew you knew because it became your pattern to be exceptionally nice, helpful, and attentive after these kinds of occurrences, as a means of making up. I convinced myself that you truly sensed the intensity of my disappointment, that you might even be afraid to behave that way again, and that you surely would take appropriate precautions from that day forward. One week later, that conjecture was blown completely to shreds.

This time it was New Year's Eve at a party in South Milwaukee, a night that is chiseled into my memory as one of the most terrifying of my life. The evening started out beautifully. We bundled the three little ones into our car, preparing for a nice family celebration with new friends and their children who lived some distance away. It was terribly cold outside that evening but toasty warm in the Scout. We drove cautiously through suburbs blanketed in newly fallen snow that sparkled under city street lights and a gauzy-white moon barely visible behind a layer of clouds. How romantic it seemed, even with the children! The forecast called for more snow, so we planned to leave the party early if necessary, not wanting to take any chances.

We arrived, and as I settled the kids down for the evening, you found your way to the kitchen where a full complement of drinks was available. It was one after another, after another, after another, as I stood with my Coke in hand, waiting for the inevitable and feeling sick inside. I kept looking anxiously at my watch, hoping it soon would be midnight so that we could leave before any embarrassing behaviors emerged. The hands would not move fast enough, and soon your actions alarmed even your friends. First your words began to slur; then you dropped your dinner plate on the floor; you raised your voice, speaking my name, putting your arm around my shoulder, and began introducing me a second time to people I had already met. Finally you lost your balance and collapsed into a chair. Following someone's suggestion, I informed our hosts that we would have to leave. I needed the help of two other guests to load you into the car, where you immediately fell asleep. I carried the children out one at a time through a whirl of snow, while apologizing to our friends as best I could. "Yes, and Happy New Year to you, too!" I nearly choked on those words, but at least I managed to return the seasonal sentiments. "Maybe," I hoped, "they do not know what is going on inside me at this moment. Maybe they think John just had too much to drink this one and only time. Maybe I will never have to see these people again in my life or those faces with their pity-laden expressions. Maybe tomorrow everything will be okay, if I can just get home, if I can get the children to bed, and if I can somehow marshall the strength to get him into the house."

I realize, John, that this is all news to you, because you never remembered any of it the very next day. You never knew about my driving us home or about the light snow that quickly turned into a blinding blizzard before I had driven five city blocks. You never saw the tears of shame that slid silently down my cheeks that night as I searched the horizon for familiar landmarks, not knowing exactly where we were and terrified that I would not find the way home. You never felt the cold wind biting into your face as you lay in the snow beside the car in our driveway, after an unsuccessful attempt to get into the house. I easily carried the children inside and put them to bed one at a time. I struggled to drag all 180 pounds of you into the house, without your offering so much as an ounce of assistance. All the time, the snow kept coming. I became overwhelmed with a fear that I could not complete the task and that you might die from exposure. I don't know why I didn't call someone to help me. It seemed to take the better part of an hour: pulling on your coat, begging you to wake up, falling down myself on the ice, pushing you, lifting one part of you at a time, before finally getting your dead-weight, limp, almost lifeless body through the back door. The back hallway steps prevented me from taking you further, but at least you were inside. I found a pillow for your head and went upstairs, too tired, too frightened, too humiliated to cry. I climbed into bed, pulling the covers up over my mouth to muffle any sound that might escape my lips. I just wanted to die!

It took me two full days to recover from that night's events, two days of re-living the nightmare, of seeing those piteous stares as I drove away in the snow, of struggling with every muscle in my body to move yours inside the house. I couldn't eat. I talked about it with a neighborhood friend who marveled at how I handled it so well. "You are amazing, Cathy. I don't know how you do it." Somehow those words made me feel that I was doing something wonderful, maybe even miraculous, by taking care of you. They should have awakened me, but I preferred the comforts of "sleep."

I never told you the details of that New Year's Eve until now. It was so hard to discuss any of these episodes with you, John, because you were always quick to point out to me that:

"The bottom line, Cath, is not how much I drink but how much I make. Have you ever stopped to consider my career, what I do for a living? I'm a lobbyist, for Christ sake! The Chamber of Commerce is making our house payments! The lumbermen paid for your car! If you don't trust me, then check it out with my bosses who know a little more than you know about what this business takes! I am not hearing any complaints or criticism from them," you'd exclaim. And you were right, of course.

"I know that, John, but it is so embarrassing. I can't stand to be in these predicaments any more. I'm afraid. Can't you understand that?" I'd ask.

"And what exactly do you have to be afraid of? I pay the bills! I buy you cars and coats! I take you out to dinner! You have charge cards to dress yourself and these kids better than anyone! So, I drink! It has never stopped me from working. In fact—if you want to know the truth, Catherine—it is *how* I work. Just don't you worry your pretty face about it. I'll tell you when to be afraid—when I can't pay the bills. Oh, what's the point of trying to explain anything to you? You'll never be satisfied no matter what I say!" Then you'd retreat to your liquor cabinet to calm yourself. So clever you were at assaulting my character.

You were very successful in your work. That was true. You were always given promotions and raises and accolades from everyone. I really couldn't understand how you were able to function, but I didn't have the energy to cope with raising the children and trying to figure it out alone. You saw the problem as my attitude rather than your behavior, and you were so convincing. I even began to believe you and felt guilty for having mentioned anything. "Maybe he's right," I'd think to myself. "Maybe I need to do more for him so that he knows that I love him and that I understand the pressure he is under." I was so confused.

You couldn't explain the DWI's, however, the times you literally lost our car, the events that caused you to be taxied home by the police or by a friend, the heavy fines you were incurring from alcohol-related traffic violations, the many nights you never came home at all—where you were, what you were doing—the times I had to pick you up from jail after your being arrested, the car accidents and related injuries to innocent people. John, what did you think about all of this? I mean, did you ever wonder what the kids or what I might have been doing or thinking when you were gone night after night, or how we would react to these serious legal matters? Did this seem okay to you? Or did you think we'd be too busy to notice?

The problem, of course, was much deeper than even the New Year's event reveals. You see, I began over time to take on a kind of "victim mentality." You can hear it in my words even now, can't you? I felt helpless, hopeless, and completely vulnerable. I didn't know what to do. My senses of empowerment and of self-esteem dissolved like snowflakes on hot coals. I simply was unable to take even the smallest action on my own behalf.

Perhaps we used poor judgment in moving to Milwaukee, so far away from the State Capitol where you actually worked. Your main employer was the Milwaukee Chamber of Commerce, we had reasoned; but the work of lobbying took place in Madison, a fact that we neglected to take into account. This wasn't a good arrangement for you, for me, or for the children. None of us benefitted as a family from your regular absences, which averaged four or five nights out of seven!

Madison, 1981

John, I really believed that the move back to Madison in January of 1981 for your new lobbying position would right all that was wrong in our lives. We had always loved Madison, the mere mention of which conjured up memories of those more playful, innocent college years. Surely, I thought, this move closer to your real place of work would make it possible for you to be home every night and for us to have dinner together as a family—to actually *be* a family again. We found a wonderful home in the country with lots of land, a pond, horses—a place where you could truly get away from it all and perhaps regain a bit of what you had as a child: the apples, raspberries, rhubarb, the barn, the tree-covered hillsides, the beautiful sunrises and sunsets. Who would want for more, I thought? Admittedly, it scared me a bit to give up the city life that I had lived for 35 years; but I was ready for a change, too, especially if the change would bring us closer together.

Changes of any kind are difficult, and I was more than a little nervous about making the adjustment after the move, especially when we arrived on that chilly January day with no carpeting upstairs and with our friends and family many miles away. We knew no one in our rural community near Token Creek and DeForest. The time-involved task of finding both playmates for the kids and acquaintances for myself was one that I had managed after all of our moves.

Knowing that I could do it again did not diminish my loneliness, however, and probably the timing was not right for you either. We started the unpacking, the arranging and picture hanging; and I finally put the children to bed after what had been an arduous day. I was exhausted from the work, the clutter, and the chaos. Anyway, when I came back downstairs, I said something that absolutely ignited you.

"I am so tired, John. It feels so lonely here. We really don't know anyone. It is so hard to do all of this again." Although quiet in nature, my tone surely revealed a touch of apprehension and maybe even depression that I could not hide. I'll never forget the next few moments.

"What *else* do you need to make you happy?" you yelled from across the room. "I've done everything for you. You've got a house in the country, your own car, and more damn stuff than any ten households put together! What else do you want? It is impossible to satisfy you!" I backed up against the wall, reaching behind me for some kind of support as you stormed out of the house toward the barn, slamming the door behind you and leaving me in stunned silence.

I did not understand your reaction! We had discussed the importance of sharing feelings in our church marriage-encounter group, and we agreed at the time on the merits of opening our lines of communication. I still don't think that my concerns were out of line. All I intended to do was to let you know what was going on inside my head and heart at the moment, but it must have sounded like more than sharing to you—more like complaining and fussing, I'm sure. As I replay that incident, not unlike so many others, it seems as if you were ready to explode and needed an event to give you permission.

Add that little scene to my "overs" list. I certainly realized after the fact that I provoked you, but did you ever consider that you may have over-reacted? I wonder whether you ever reflected on these kinds of episodes or whether they were simply forgotten the next day. If you were concerned about not being able to make me happy, why didn't you tell me that? Why didn't you ask what I wanted? I would have told you. Instead, once again you saw yourself as a good husband in buying the perfect house for me and the children, and you saw me as the perfectly thankless wife. It is hard for me to see how you could have come to that conclusion, especially if you had taken the time to think about it. I had to make a major adjustment to manage remote, country living—one that required advance planning for everything from groceries to haircuts to dental appointments. Every trip into Madison with the kids seemed like a major expedition at first. Still, I was mindful of wanting to do things for you, surprising you with funny gifts at your office and arranging for special birthday celebrations at the Madison Club. Do you remember the camel-hair coat that I bought you from some of my first business profits? It was the one you lost on that unplanned trip to Las Vegas, while I was still paying off the bill, by the way. I didn't appreciate that, but I did appreciate you. You must have known it. Why else would I stay? Well, there's not much I can do about it now.

Life was not easy that first year in the country—very lonely, to be more precise—but there were some unexpected and wonderful times. Remember the pony we bought? That was your idea, and the kids absolutely loved him. They fed and cared for him, learning how to assume responsibility. I had hoped that our second and fully grown horse would awaken in you the kind of joy you had as a child. Yet, you rarely rode Wisco and were never sober on those few occasions when you did take him out for exercise. There's one image, I confess, that is so funny when I think about it now. You went out to ride him one day after a few too many Bloody Mary's, neglecting to tighten his belly strap sufficiently. I looked up from the kitchen window to see you coming around the barn, having slipped completely off to Wisco's side! Whenever someone talks to me about riding side-saddle, a grin always breaks across my face. It was so comical—just like in a cartoon or something! None of that sobered you up, though. I don't know where I got the idea that some horses and a farm house would diminish your need for alcohol. I flatly denied that you were addicted, that your body needed it, even though I grew increasingly more disgusted with the drinking. I denied it to myself, and I covered for you with nearly everyone.

I started my story-telling for you, John, in part because I couldn't face the reality of what it would mean for me and the children if I actually admitted that you had a disease. It was not just any disease, but a seriously debilitating one that might cost you your career if it were widely known. Lying became my protective shield. When I altered the facts, it always felt like I was protecting the kids, your mother and sister, and my family. I believed that I was protecting you, too, when I spoke with your employers, making up excuses for your absence or lateness or behavior. I wonder now whether any of them ever believed me. How could they have? They must have seen me as part of the problem, and I guess I was. I was denying it, enabling it, and—worst of all—covering it up.

Maybe my dishonesty was born out of embarrassment, out of fear of what was happening, out of not knowing what I could do. I know I worried about money and about whether I could afford to live without your income. I don't know what gave me the idea that I had the power to change you, to fix you, or to help you; but I did. I really thought I could do it. Meanwhile, you were out of sorts—no, you were *drunk* for parent-teacher conferences. You were *drunk* for the children's birthday parties. You were *drunk* when serving as the auctioneer at the Pumpkin Hollow School fund-raiser, when we were entertaining friends at the Madison Club, and when our mothers came to visit for Mother's Day. I eventually decided to avoid as many social occasions as possible. That was my only means of averting the feelings of fear and nausea in the pit of my stomach that engulfed me as those occasions approached, along with images of your drunkenness and my humiliation.

Why did I stay? Well, John, there were some pretty good "perks" with your work. Those family trips to Arizona, Georgia, Tennessee, and Florida—all expenses paid—seemed to soothe the wounds. I know that I'm not imagining it. We really did have fun, and the children still look back on those experiences with such fondness. I loved seeing them all so happy. In those environments, I felt appreciated and relished the pampering. I found pleasure in playing my role as your partner at the major events, being as comfortable with small talk among strangers as you were. We all felt kind of rewarded on those encapsulated occasions, and the family feelings often lasted for many weeks after we returned home. I must admit that as bad as things were, I always held onto my belief that somehow, someday we would get our relationship and our family back on track. I believed that both of us really wanted that more than anything.

I wonder sometimes why people we knew so well never said anything to us. Maybe it is best that they didn't, as more than likely we wouldn't have been receptive to any advice, much less to any criticism. Furthermore, let's face it, it was *our* problem. I know that your sister and mother worried a great deal, but what could they have done? People in our church in DeForest expressed their concern, as did the pastor, now that I think about it. I really believed that your decision to join the church choir was a good sign, a signal that you wanted to change and that you needed something to fill the void in your life that alcohol created. You truly filled the church, John, with your voice. I was hoping for a miracle from God. That was when I still believed in you and in us.

That church did a lot to help me. I thoroughly enjoyed singing in the choir, teaching Sunday school, planning fund-raisers, and creating other projects that I literally threw myself into, probably to get away from the misery at home. I wish that I would have confided in someone. After all, no one there ever passed judgment on you or us. I wasn't honest, and I regret that. I made up some lame excuse about your going through a period of doubt to explain your absence from choir practice. I just couldn't say, "John is out getting drunk right now," or "John has a hangover," or "John is passed out on the living room floor." I was too ashamed. I was sure that people would be shocked and then think less of both of us or pity me. I didn't think I could handle that.

Finally, I lost the strength to handle anything anymore and made an appointment to speak with a NewStart counselor after seeing an advertisement on television. Initially, I was even untruthful with her, claiming that I was there to deal with issues from my childhood instead of admitting that I was there because of you. Thankfully, the counselor knew better and as the sessions continued, the truth finally did come out. For a very long time, I was not frank or honest with our children either about the severity or even the name of your problem. I managed to keep it from them—and the whole family, I thought—for years. I realized too late that they knew about it all along. NewStart helped the children and me realize that alcoholism *is* a disease. Furthermore, I learned that your having three loving children, a devoted wife, and a promising career was not a cure. Our only hope was medical and therapeutic treatment.

TREATMENT I—OUTPATIENT, 1985

I felt your anger, John, in the fall of 1985, when you were given the ultimatum by the court for either jail or outpatient treatment, after another in a string of DWI's. Given those alternatives, you were persuaded to go; but nothing could convince you that you needed help. Thank heavens for your mother (she was 72 at the time!) who offered to care for the children so that you and I could attend the mandatory, 4-hour evening program for recovering alcoholics and their spouses. That experience was hard for you—humbling, more accurately. If it's any consolation, it was equally humbling for me. I had to open up in front of all of those strangers and admit that our life was virtually a nightmare rather than the perfect picture that I wanted it to be. I hated that and resented having to go! I really did not understand for a long time that the program was there to support not just alcoholics but family members as well. Moreover, I really didn't believe that I needed help or fixing.

Unfortunately, within a year and a half, your sobriety gave way to regular drinking and to the agonizingly familiar routine: another DWI, another arrival at one of Kristin's high school performances drunk, and another visit to a therapist. In June of 1987, you were given orders for a month of *inpatient* treatment, and once more you were furious with me. I know you must remember that night when you got the call giving you that second ultimatum for treatment and sobriety, which now were stipulations of employment. That threat seemed to provide the motivation you needed.

Your anger was so intense initially that even the doctor was concerned for the physical safety of the children and me. He suggested that I take them away for the evening so as not to risk injury. Still, I could not be honest with them or with our families. I never told either of our parents where we were going or why. I just took the kids to the Holiday Inn, telling them that we were going to have a mini vacation. "Any more than that would be impossible for them to comprehend," I thought. "How do I tell children who absolutely adore their father that he might be a danger to them? How do I say those words without their losing respect or love for him? Moreover, if he gets over this someday, why would they ever have to know?" I can still picture them playing in the pool and having a wonderful time. I imagined that they were totally oblivious as to the severity of your condition.

I know now that they were keenly aware of our dilemma, reading my face perhaps and noting other signs that indicated your inability to remain sober. Kristin first realized you had a drinking problem when she was 11, confiding her fears to her fifth-grade teacher. By age 13, she attended NewStart meetings with the boys and me, learning among other things that the illness was life-threatening. Why did I think that I had hidden this from the children? Of course they knew. Perhaps the better question is: Why couldn't I talk about the problem with them openly? Why did I feel I needed to keep up a good front? I realize that Turmos coped best by "stuffing it," carefully putting all unpleasantries out of sight, out of mind. This was my legacy, one I'm trying now to break.

I nearly suffocated with anxiety as I sat near the pool that hot, humid June night, contemplating what horrors the children and I would face when we returned home the next day. We were all shocked to find a very apologetic note from you on the kitchen counter, explaining that you were going again for treatment and that you loved us all. My heart melted. Once again, I wanted so much to believe that *this time* it would work.

Treatment II—Inpatient, 1987

While you were undergoing hospital treatment, John, I kept it a secret again from most of our family and friends. It was easy to do because you were gone so frequently anyway. I took time to reread your old Vietnam letters while you were gone, trying to fall in love again because the flame had gone out long ago. There you were for me: wanting to make me happy, telling me about reading every book you could get your hands on, wishing the days would disappear, saying that your friends in the barracks all wanted to meet me, that photos of my paintings were displayed on the wall for all to see, how you dreamed about Hawaii, how you couldn't wait to hold me once more, and often ending with your special salutation, "ja elska da." I hoped that you would return strong and ready to rebuild our family—just as you returned after that longest of years ready to begin our life together.

That was the end of June and early July, and what followed were four nearly perfect years, truly the best years I can ever remember. The treatment program went well. You lived in your own apartment in July when you were released from the hospital, got up every morning to attend 7:00 A.M. group sessions for AA through the month of August, and eventually moved back home in September. You continued to progress. You came home for dinner each evening after work, cared for the horses for the very first time, and even began to look like your old self again with a healthy pallor returning to your face. Our life stabilized, became predictable, and was actually fun. You went on horseback rides with Nels and Lars, instructing them on handling technique. We sang again in the church choir, staying after Sunday services to chat with neighbors. You delighted Kristin with euchre lessons and Risk strategies. You attended school functions totally sober, making the children ever so proud. We celebrated birthdays and other special occasions at the Madison Club, where the wait staff—sensitive to your needs—prepared you special nonalcoholic drinks and treated the children like members of the family. Ours were the only children of lobbyists to experience these ring-side seats where their father worked and enjoyed complete respect. We all began to relax finally as the school year came to a close—one full school year for the children without incident. We almost forgot there had been a problem. We were completely unprepared for the events to follow.

THE RELAPSE, 1988

It happened in a way that seems rather predictable and quite preventable now. You were sent on a business trip to Reno, Nevada, a city known to have more than a few distractions. A recovering alcoholic being sent to Reno and expecting him not to drink? Did your employers think that you needed some kind of road test? Maybe they truly didn't know how difficult this would be for you or how vulnerable you still were. In retrospect, why did I even *let* you go? I knew that this was like handing a book of matches to a pyromaniac. Why didn't I go along, if it were important for you to be there? True, I had arranged to vacation in northern Wisconsin with the children to be with Liz's family, as we had done for so many summers. Keeping that commitment, however, was surely not as important as keeping you healthy. Everyone would have understood. I believe now that you needed more support than either of us was willing to admit. In any regard, after you returned, I phoned from the lake to hear about Reno but heard instead the all-too-familiar sound in your inebriated voice. "Oh, no, John. Please don't tell me you've given up," I whispered so that the children and Liz would not hear.

"Don't worry, Cath. Believe me, this was the wake-up call I needed. I'm okay, just a little tired," you said, hoping to cover up what had transpired. You claimed later that the experience of drinking again was a real scare, just a relapse and no more; but I knew better. Liz could see it in my face.

"Well, what happened now?" she wanted to know.

"Nothing. John just isn't feeling well, and he has to leave right away for Lakelawn for more business," I offered as a half-true, hopefully reasonable, response. I simply could not talk about it with her. She'd tell me to leave, to get divorced, and to get on with my life. I did not want to hear it. I knew she never really could understand. Her life was so predictable, so comfortable, so unlike mine in every way. I remember that as a child, all I ever wanted was to be like Liz. As an adult, I could see that the contrast between the two of us could not have been greater.

Well, at least I took what I considered to be my first brave step. I told you that you would have to break the news of your drinking to the children. You had to take responsibility for your actions, the counselors had instructed me. I did not, however, inform your employers, preferring to trust that you really meant what you had said: This was a "wake-up call"—nothing more. And, John, you were sober much of the time for the next three years. Again our family was reunited. We had experiences together that even Walt Disney would find so hard to believe.

The Second Relapse, 1989

Of course, no one knew—absolutely no one—about the second relapse less than a year later. It occurred during another out-of-town trip—this one, a company reward for professional achievements and sobriety. You were invited to travel with the Governor's staff to Norway in March. I remember thinking to myself that although they were right to congratulate you in this manner, I should have been invited, too. John, you knew that it had been a life-long dream of *mine* to go to Norway and to go with *you*. We had talked about it for more than two decades, and I felt hurt for having been left out of the equation. I wondered if I would ever matter to you or if I would ever be acknowledged for standing by you. I didn't need a parade, but neither did I need the rain. A "Thank you, Cath, for being there for me," would have been just fine. I just needed something.

It sounds selfish in retrospect. I wish that I had been more appreciative of how hard you were working to remain sober. I could have congratulated you and sent you off with all my love. Instead I seethed with a jealous anger. When you phoned from that bar in the Copenhagen airport to tell me that your return flight would be delayed, I recognized the familiar slur in your voice, the music in the background, and knew you were drinking again. In less than two year's time, I feared that we might now be back to square one. You arrived home with wonderful gifts for the children and for me, a tradition that softened the sadness caused by your long absences for business travel. We never discussed my feelings or your drinking. I hoped that the episode was just a slip-up, not a true set-back;

but deep down, I believe that I knew it was more than that. "Why else," I might have asked myself, "did I have these recurring fantasies about receiving a phone call and hearing that you'd been killed in a plane crash or a car accident?" "News" that might bring grief to most seemed instead to calm my fears. "People would respond with sympathy and kindness to this kind of tragedy," I imagined. "They never would have to know everything. I would make it somehow and then begin to live again." These kinds of thoughts began to confuse and frighten me. Did I love you? If I didn't, why was I so concerned about your sobriety? Was I starting to let go?

I also became concerned about the person I was becoming, someone who felt hostile, cynical, and critical. I had always been described as a Pollyanna, the one who made others laugh with clever comments, who melted the coldest stare with a special glance. "Catherine, you absolutely light up the room with your presence," one of your employers had said to me. "You are John's greatest asset," said another. I was the one who created beautiful gift baskets out of bows and bric-a-brac, but it was my interpersonal skills that made the difference. Little did I realize that slowly my most important personal attribute was being displaced by bitterness and fear.

At other times, I managed to push my anger aside to enjoy the moment. Probably the best of those times was a vacation we planned with another family, a true vacation that had no relationship to your work. You arranged it all, so rich in memories of your youth, a week's cruise on a 40-foot boat down the Mississippi. You recalled your childhood on the river and built camp-fires on sandbars where we sat around telling ghost stories until late at night. We docked in small towns for ice cream cones, held onto the ropes so that we could safely navigate the locks, had ham-and-eggs breakfasts accompanied by the hum of the motor, the chatter of nuthatches, and beautiful sunrises. We relaxed, laughed, sang the old ballads, ate fresh fish dinners, and fell asleep to the sound of river waters lapping up against the boat. You were healthy, happy, totally calm on a river that gave you a certain sense of freedom. You loved facing the elements, but this was more than that. The Mississippi was a source of peace, your friend, your home. All of us could see it in your face. Those memories at this writing cause me to wonder why we never considered going back to a simpler life. That was where we started. That was what brought us together. It might have made a difference. I guess I'll always be wondering what might have—could have—made the difference we needed.

Those four years after treatment were nearly perfect. I came upon an occasional beer can in the basement and noticed just a faint hint of alcohol on your breath from time to time. Ever so often, you'd come home later than expected, and then there would be a phone call where I could hear that barely perceptible lilt. I worried, but I convinced myself that you had won your battle with alcohol. I realized too late, of course, that you had just become more clever at disguising it.

During this time period, your lobbying career was at its peak. You developed a strong reputation over the years as one who could predict the votes 100%. You related equally well with Democrats and

Republicans. You acquired a class that worked well with those from bigger cities, but you never lost touch with country folk who felt with you a special kinship. You could adjust your language from complex to simple, charming legislators with stories and attention until they made a verbal commitment to vote according to your wishes. Phillip Morris couldn't have been happier with the pay-offs, cigarette taxes kept to only five cents! Not to mention the State Savings & Loan that profited from your successful lobbying for deregulation. It was hard work and lots of pressure. But you loved it, every minute; and you loved the praise and rewards that followed. You made me a believer, John.

Then one Christmas came a revelation from you that truly startled me. I can picture it now. The children were outside playing with their friends in the whitest of snows that can only be found in the country on a wintry-high, blue-sky, sunshiny day. The horses grazed on fresh hay that you had unbaled and thrown in their trough. Flour dust still covered my hands and long blue-jean skirt from preparing the pies for Christmas dinner. You were reading comfortably in your chair, smoking a cigarette with that pensive expression that periodically veiled your face. The fire in the fireplace filled the room with a radiant warmth and a seasonal scent of pine. Christmas carols from your father's old radio completed the moment, playing softly in the background behind the clatter of assorted roasters and a bevy of baking pans.

You turned to me and remarked, "If I drink again, it will kill me. I know that." A lump suddenly grew in my throat, making it almost impossible for me to speak. Then I said, almost in a whisper, "Yes, John, I know that, too." Our eyes met, searching intently across the room for some kind of visual reassurance that everything would be okay. I knew then that you had changed. My prayers had been answered! Never in the previous 20 years had you acknowledged openly how dangerous was the path you had been following. I was now certain that you would *never* drink again. No more did I need the phone call fantasy.

And you were almost completely sober, John, for months to come. During this whole time period, you were the man I married. Everyone could see it and expressed their relief and happiness to both of us. The children and I will always cherish those years. They confirmed what we were beginning to doubt ourselves: that you really were the best dad in the world, a most loving and generous husband, and the most talented lobbyist whom those in the State Capitol had ever known! There were a few more trips to attractive places like Naples and Nashville. The best part for all of us, John, was that you were there to share it! I allowed myself to get lost in those romantic surroundings, convinced for the moment that life would work out just as planned. After we returned home in January from our last trip together, I realized that it was only a matter of time until everything would collapse upon us.

I don't remember any other good times. The Gulf War in '91 brought back terrible memories for you, as well as your nightmares and the uncontrollable jerking as you slept. You talked about the snakes and the rats and your fears for Nels and Lars, should they ever be drafted. This seemed so strange to me as you never mentioned anything about the war—not in letters then or in conversations later—that would explain these behaviors. I wonder now if you were having anxiety-ridden dreams for another reason. It was not long after peace was restored in the Middle East that you came to my painting studio one day and announced out of nowhere: "I don't think I have what it takes to be your husband." John, there were times when I would have given anything for you to have left us, when I fantasized—as I mentioned before—about your dying in a car accident and getting the life insurance. Yet, that spring your words for some reason sent me into a complete state of panic.

"What are you talking about?" I asked, totally shocked and unprepared for this conversation. "We've spent so much time trying to make things work!" I tried desperately to think of something to say, something to make you reconsider the decision, hoping you would take back those incomprehensible words. "And what do you mean by 'what it takes to be my husband'?" I wondered out loud. "All I've needed is for you to be here."

"I just don't think it is working for me. That's all. Don't read anything else into it. It isn't that complicated," you said in a matter-of-fact way with no added inflection in your voice.

"You mean you just want to flick it all in? Why can't we talk or at least think about it for a while?" I asked, hoping to stall for time or that time could repair the damage. I wanted us to reach some kind of consensus. "Just tell me that you'll think about it, John. Or is there another woman? Please tell me if that's it. That I can understand. I need to know what has changed," I pleaded.

I felt certain that you must not have been telling me everything because it just didn't make any sense. Just months before, you had announced that you knew that another drink would kill you. You seemed to be so much happier and were clearly healthier than you had been in years. Now out of the clear blue you suddenly were saying to me that you didn't want this kind of life. Did that mean that you missed the alcohol? Was our relationship too boring? Did it feel to you that the good times were passing you by? What was it? It just didn't register.

You insisted that there was no other woman in the picture, but I still wondered about that. There was Stephanie, your assistant, who showed up that time in Orlando to my surprise but not to yours. I also remember dismissing Mary's concerns years ago about your fidelity, after she reported seeing you with another woman at some kind of athletic banquet. That really does not make sense, does it? At the very least, I should have asked you for an explanation. Men just don't leave home for no reason; and when they do leave, most go to someone else. I don't even want to think about your having been unfaithful to me, but I have to face the facts that clearly point in that direction. You should have told me. I wouldn't have made it easy, but that's not the point. A reason would have made it easier for all of us in the long run. I seem to have been more than passive about too many things. Probably another "overs list" item.

There were a few times when I did ask for explanations but then had to listen to your accusations of my not being trusting or grateful for all of your hard work. I never actually had a "smoking gun," and that made it impossible for me to get any place with those ridiculous conversations. Women really weren't the problem, even if you had dozens of other women. Neither were job or family stressors. The problem again was alcohol. I began to direct more of my attention toward my business and away from you and the children when I realized that I would soon be on my own. I needed to build something secure before our life completely crumbled. A part of me absolutely refused to believe you really meant what you said, that you didn't want to be my husband any longer. It took me a long time to accept the fact that you really had made a final decision, and you made it when you were sober.

November of 1991

Not long after that first announcement, you came home with another one that was far more devastating. I was in the kitchen with Nels and Lars, discussing their equipment needs for the Thanksgiving ski holiday in Oregon with Liz's family. Kristin was still at school, having stayed late for play practice. The four of us had planned to attend the opening night performance that weekend together. Suddenly you came to us from your chair in the living room, sat down, and spoke.

"I don't want to be here anymore." Just like that, in front of the boys, you announced that you were leaving, adding later for absolute clarity, "I am never going to live in this house again."

I sensed that a most important and difficult discussion was about to take place, and I quickly determined that it might be easier if the boys left the room. I gave them some money to get their ski equipment; and without needing any further explanation, they reached for their jackets and were immediately on their way.

"John, please, I need to understand this," I said as calmly as I could under the circumstances. Seeing no change of heart and hearing no words of regret, I began to cry. "Please don't leave," I begged.

"Don't go into your histrionics, Catherine. I've made my decision, and that's it!" you stated emphatically. I could see your neck artery pulsing as your face reddened and your eyes widened, causing me to freeze in position as I let myself absorb your message.

"Where will you go? How can we reach you? What should I say to your mother?" I asked, hoping that these questions might startle you into rethinking your decision.

"When I know, I'll tell you. Say whatever you want to whomever you want. I really don't care right now," and out of the door you went. Nels and Lars came back home an hour or so later, hoping they would see your car in the driveway. They never even had a chance to say good-bye, just came in the house quietly, knowing what must have transpired, and went silently up to their rooms. None of us could talk. I picked up Kristin from her practice, and told her about your decision after we came home. She took her school books and her heavy heart upstairs, too, where she could cry alone.

An amazing sense of peace came over our home that day. For more than six months, we'd all been "walking on egg shells" to some extent, not really knowing how our story would end. We knew that never again would we have to live with the uncertainties that had become so commonplace in the past. That book chapter was finished. The boys and I attended Kristin's play that weekend, noticing the effects of alcohol as you entered. Already you seemed like a stranger to me. To the children, it was different. You were still their father, the one who had taken them on long hikes through nearby woods, finding each the perfect walking stick for wacking their way through the weeds. You were the one who had corralled their energies to transform our front lawn into a menagerie for Halloween night, complete with huge mechanized spiders that crawled on our front bay windows to scare trick-or-treaters. You were the one who had taken the children out driving through uncharted fields, removing the top of the Bronco so they could feel the sweet summer breezes. They loved the trips back to Crawford County with the "I-remember-when" stories from your teenage years. Skiing together during winter vacation, picnics outside when the weather permitted, big bonfires in the back yard on cool fall evenings, so many good times jewel their recollections. How could they say good-bye? They couldn't, and neither could I.

I'm not sure exactly what I was thinking that day you announced your final departure. Maybe I was afraid to be divorced or was apprehensive about the process. I was right about that for sure, if anything only underestimating how vulnerable I would become. Maybe I doubted whether I could afford to send the kids to college. John, you brought such turmoil to my life but also so much joy. I still wanted you. I could not let you go without begging you to stay. Maybe it was because I had not been honest with the rest of the world—our families, in particular—about how we were doing. I never told any of them about your relapse or let them know that our marriage had been more than fragile for years. When you left that day, John, I told the kids that you just needed a time-out, but they knew better. Only within the last few months did I learn that they all knew far more than I had imagined. I was so self-absorbed that I missed their awareness, certain that I had shielded them from everything. I should have known better. Our children had radar-sharp sensors that told them when you were drinking and how I was feeling. That's all the information they needed to guess what lay ahead. Anti-depressants got me through, as did Mom, who always has been there for me. Why did I want you to stay when you made it perfectly clear that you wanted to leave? Maybe I could not face the fact that we, that I, had failed. Or stated more clearly in terms that you can understand, John, maybe I could not accept the fact that I had no return for the investment of my time.

That was November of 1991. Thanksgiving, always a big family event at our house, was a day that I just wanted behind me. Nels and Lars were in Oregon, while Kristin remained at home with me and Mom. None of us was excited about Christmas either, until you called to say that you wanted to come over with some gifts. You seemed like a stranger to me when you walked in the door, but the kids were so excited in an apprehensive kind of way. They probably sensed my ambivalence, not knowing for sure how I would react. The last thing they wanted was more hostility, more angry looks, more clenched jaws, more negativity. It must have been difficult for you, too, to come into this house that was once your home. You gave each of us a card with $100.00. I was angry and cynical about the whole "gifts" gesture at the time, just as the kids probably predicted, but now I feel such sadness as I review that day in my mind's eye. I know you did love us all once, and that was your way of trying to make certain that we knew it.

You were so like your father, John, in that regard, but nowhere near as wise. He would never have been so arrogant as to claim he that had all of life's answers. More important, he knew the one question among the many that totally eluded you: "What is life all about?" You never figured that one out, did you? It is relationships—human relationships, between friends and family members—that makes life meaningful, purposeful, and satisfying. And good relationships require time and energy and work! Your father would have stayed. I really believe that.

Shortly afterwards, we began the paperwork for the divorce. That was not fun. By the time we began the procedure, I was no longer emotionally connected to you. I was financially dependent, however, and soon I realized exactly how vulnerable the children and I were. Never again—right up to and including this very day—would we ever feel we had enough financial security to plan more than a week at a time.

I am glad that I had Basketree Gifts to carry us through for basic necessities. That little business is still in its building phase, so I have had to pour the profits right back in to make the company grow. Not to mention that I had problems with my partner there as well. Carol and I "divorced," so to speak, when her primary career demands grew. I was fortunate eventually in finding a new partner, who not only handled those business details that I am so famous for overlooking, but who also brought me her maturity and warmth out of which a wonderful friendship has grown. Jan and I invested even more time in the business, banking on it to support our families. I do not regret that strategic decision, but I do realize that the children have paid the price. I could not be there for them all of the time. It seemed that Kristin was able to manage any responsibility handed to her, for her capacity to cope was fine-tuned by this time. The boys were younger, less mature, and a very different story. If you had been there, John, it would have helped us all. I simply couldn't do it all myself. The boys, in particular, needed a father. Super Mom *plus* Dad I was not.

It was hard explaining to Nels why you didn't come to see him in the hospital after his car accident. It seemed ironic that you couldn't be there for him: the one who had such admiration for you, who was like you and understood you, who shared your work ethic, who envisioned a partnership—"Forde & Forde, Lobbyists," he imagined—hoping to work with you someday, and who even understood your sadness. He assumed adult responsibilities when you left, becoming the man I could lean on and depend on, perhaps too much so. His childhood ended sooner than it should have. He sensed well before I did that our story would not have a happy ending. So perceptive was he that at times we both forgot that he was still a teenager. Part of that forgetting included his becoming more and more detached from school, from friends, and from me.

It was hard for us to understand why you came "self-medicated" the night of Kristin's next play, during her senior year, and why you brought your "associate," Stephanie. Similar behavior at Kristin's evening baccalaureate service revealed to all present that your condition had not improved. I was relieved that you were under control for the graduation ceremony the following afternoon so as not to be embarrassed again; but I was anxious, nonetheless. I couldn't be certain of Kristin's reaction. She kept any thoughts or fears or embarrassment to herself, a preference that contributed to creating a barrier between us—just when we needed each other most. I lacked the skill needed to break through it, imagining that it might disappear on its own accord someday, I guess. Kristin appeared to be so "together." I wanted the appearance to be the reality. I was so glad that your mother came to her ceremony and happier still that she stayed overnight in our new home for the party the next day. I am sure that she must have decided long ago that you were no longer her responsibility; she was still the children's grandmother, however, and she wanted to be there for these kinds of occasions for them. She was right, of course, but still I wanted her understanding, her forgiveness perhaps, or some reassurance that she did not blame me. Maybe that was too much to expect from a woman who was probably still feeling hurt herself.

It has been especially difficult for Lars. He began making many choices that changed his life forever, and how many times I wished you were there in a fully functioning frame of mind to help me deal with all of this. He was in court for truancy, loitering, and underage smoking. He found school so aversive that he stopped going altogether, finally earning his diploma at an alternative school. Most difficult was a relationship that both boys established with a single parent in town, who seemed to have made it her mission in life to rescue young boys who were unhappy. I really didn't know what happened at her house, but she made it known that teens could use her home as a hiding place from the world, in general, or from school, in particular. Ours were among many kids who skipped school, taking refuge there. As you know, Lars became intimately involved with her daughter. The alternative high school allowed him to work so that he could afford the expenses that came with being a single parent at the age of 17. I was so glad that you were able to see Lars again and your granddaughter. It meant the world to all of us, but especially to Lars whom you hadn't even seen for the better part of a year. He is a most sensitive, attentive father, which makes me so proud. At the same time, my heart aches as I picture the struggle he will always face and the simpler life he will never know. He is now learning a great deal the hard way, but he is learning; and at the same time, he continues to pursue his double passions of art and music. We must be grateful for what he is doing and spend less time lamenting for what he cannot have.

Once Kristin moved downtown to campus, she always enjoyed having the opportunity to see you, and especially at the Paradise Lounge. Everyone there treated you and her like family. "Little John," they called her. She was always so proud of you. She amazes me, John. Where did she get this intelligence, this beauty, this grace? When she received her University award, I realized that I have not embellished her attributes one bit. She really is outstanding; but she does bear too great a burden, I fear. I see it sometimes in her eyes. When she is not prepared for someone to mention you or to ask about you, tears begin to well, her lip quivers, and pink blushes fill her cheeks. At other times, she anticipates those feelings and leaves the room before losing her composure. She holds herself together very well most of the time, but those unplanned-for moments tell me she is hurting inside. I wish I could help her more. I worry that she tried to play my role after we separated, looking after you as best she could. If that is the case, then we have a great deal more in common than either of us realized. She had a very special relationship with you, John, the kind most daughters would love to experience with their fathers. She knows that I have not always shared her unconditional love for you, however, and that makes the kind of conversation we need to have almost impossible. What she does not know is how much I need her now—her strength and understanding, her forgiveness and love. Maybe as time goes on, we will be able to talk again. I do have faith that we will.

The children do not talk to me very often about you, perhaps because they know my feelings toward you have lost their tenderness. I must confess that I'm not really sure why. I'm afraid at times that they harbor a sizable resentment toward me. At other times, I convince myself that they must know how hard I tried. They must understand that our futures depended on the success of my business, which depended entirely on me. They must realize that although I erred in choosing to hide your illness, I did so believing that I was protecting them. They must know how much I love them. I wonder if they know how much I still hurt inside. Thankfully, the anger finally is beginning to diminish.

I wish that I hadn't been cut off from nearly all Forde family communications, a common result of divorce, I know. The recent family reunion was both wonderful and awkward at the same time—few knowing exactly what to say, with the noted exception of your cousin Lars. He still hurts as we do, John. Perhaps some of your family blame me for your illness. I might have tried harder with them if I had sensed some degree of understanding or compassion. Your sister and mother are kidding themselves if they think I didn't try to help you. But then, I haven't told them what they probably needed to know: the car accidents, the DWI's, the nights in jail, the humiliation suffered time and time again because of your behavior in church, in private homes, in public bars, and more. Shielding them from all of that has only contributed to my hurt in the long run. It is entirely possible that none of us knows how to begin a conversation. Perhaps Clarice, your mother, and I will acquire the courage to try again some day and then to put all of these feelings of anger to rest. Of course, I always thought that you and I would talk again some day.

It was probably a mistake on my part not to attend your niece's wedding. Actually, it is more honest to admit that it *was* a mistake. I acted inappropriately when Clarice sent the invitation just days before, even if she did so only at your prompting. I don't know why I didn't see your intentions or hers as honorable, maybe even forgiving. You were right. Kim was still my niece, regardless of our marital status. I still remember entertaining her at our Chicago apartment when she was just 5 years old. She was so excited by the whole adventure, and such fun we had with her on her first overnight away from home. I wish I had thought more about those memories and important ties before acting so hastily and selfishly. I must apologize. Relationships. Relationships are what life is all about. And I may have damaged this one beyond repair.

I need to catch my breath before I continue, John. I have an easier time writing about some times and details than about others. This all still seems too close, too painful. When I feel this way, I reach again for your letters, hoping that you might say something to me that gets me through the moment. Often, I find a bit of irony.

Love,

Catherine

Ft. Leonard Wood, Mo.
December 11, 1966

Dear Cathy,

140 hrs. to go and we can count the days on one hand and it's really great. . . . . . Basic is all over!! We are through with all our tests and this week we have nothing to do but a few exercises and drilling-so the week will probably go pretty slow. We graduate Friday morning and leave at 6 A.M. Sat.

Have nothing to write except I love you more than ever. That's the one thing I've gotten out of basic-knowing that I love you more than ever and all I want is to try to make you happy.

Send my love,

John

An Khe, Vietnam
July 6, 1967

Hi,

Just got your letter written in green type, where you told about the problem with the narrow minded goody goody and perhaps too-young counselor. First of all, now you have kind of an idea of what Basic training was like, in that there was absolutely no one to talk to about anything. . . I was afraid that after two-years exposure to people like that, I would come out of the army a complete moron. Which is why I'm so happy to be situated where I am. . . . I think I have a general idea of your problem there. Although you didn't say it in so many words, guess that part of your frustration is . . . . over all their attitudes. . . . which in turn is . . . the biggest problem that all the Christian denominations have and that is the tendency to be quite self-centered. It seems that as soon as a person goes thru the tumultuous decision on the question of religion, that once they finally accept Christ, they spend the rest of their days worrying only about their own spiritual life. But because "we are judged by our works" they go to work for their church. And pretty soon everyone is tied up in fighting among themselves, teaching "church" doctrines instead of thinking about basic Christianity—and we have the Catholic-Lutheran "most beautiful church" competition, and "the Baptists will go to hell so we have to convert them" and in effect, Christians associate with Christians, argue religious beliefs among themselves, rationalize away the "good works" law by serving coffee after services, and rationalize the missionary bit away by inviting a Catholic into the house once a month. . . they worry about themselves and their church, forgetting that Christians as a whole are in the minority. . . . I am very pleased that my soon-to-be-wife is frustrated with narrow-minded people—actively.

ja elska da forever—Love

John

Vietnam
Oct. 30, 1967

Dear Cathy,

Just received your letter written last Monday after your traumatic Sunday. . . it is silly of you to ask if I'm still willing to try it with you. You know the answer to that. But to be truthful, I'm glad that it all happened. . . because it did make you sit down and think everything out. . . . How many times have I told you, probably most of the time not very tactfully, that you are too sensitive and worry too much about other people and not enough about yourself. I'm sorry. . . I lose my temper. . . Your sensitivity and warmth, and love for everyone is part of your real charm, and why I love you. But it has to be regulated. . . . The thing that makes me mad is that you've let these people step on you, depress you, and make you lose confidence. . . . With your personality and talent you have no right to say that you lack self respect or confidence. Gibran says, "Know your own true worth, and you shall not perish. Reason is your light and your beacon of truth." . . . I guess I sound like I know it all. I don't but I know you and love you more than anything. I can't stand to see you allowing yourself to be hurt. It's time you built up a defense against it. . . We'll soon be together. The time can't come fast enough.

ja elska da-

John

Vietnam
Jan. 25, 1968

Dear Cath–

There's nothing quite so black as Vietnam when there is no moon. . . . I should be writing every day happy thoughts about you because that's how I really feel when I think of the future. . . . when I think of our life together. . . . All I want is to make you happy. I get sick when I think of you being anything but–(which brings flashbacks of all the hard times we had at school because of me and all I can say is "thank God you are still there"). The point is I'm afraid my daily letters are far from happy notes–. . . The biggest problem is that my nerves are shot. Being in a base camp like I am–we have no time for thought of an offense but think purely defense –and we sit and wait. It gets terribly tense and nerves are strung to the breaking point. . . .

Cath–I love you–and the word "love" takes on more meaning everyday. When I make you unhappy, kick me, because it's the last thing I want.

ja elska da

John

CHAPTER 5

A FAMILY IN CRISIS

Treatment Failure and Final Separation

June 2, 1997

Dear John,

You surprised us all during Christmas of 1994, by delivering small gifts to everyone when none of us was home. Soon afterwards, we were notified that your mother was hospitalized in Viroqua. Kristin and I drove there to see her, and I can't tell you how grateful I was for the chance to tell her finally that I loved her. She did the same, but she really wanted to see you. Within a week—January 11, to be exact—our granddaughter, Shiloh, came into the world. I couldn't hide it from anyone any longer. I was indeed a grandmother. You may not remember that date because none of us could find you to tell you. Evidently, a friend of yours told you about having read it in the newspaper. I can understand why you were angry for having been left out of the loop. Believe me, please; it was not intentional. We all assumed that someone else in the family had called to share the good news with you. None realized that all of us had failed to make contact. That was why I arranged to see you shortly afterwards, in addition to my needing to know how you were. We had not seen each other for quite a long time, several months at least. I wanted to see you, to know how work was going. I never could stop worrying.

That scene when we last met is one that I will carry with me forever. It is not on my "overs" list, thankfully. I want to keep it exactly as it was. I hope my words can paint the picture I have in my mind. I'll try.

You wanted to meet in a place where you would be comfortable, a public place with people quietly talking and laughing, completing a kind of familiar social backdrop perhaps, one with a few distractions: the Paradise Lounge, of course, your home away from home. I was always nervous before these appointments with you, not knowing whether we would have a calm conversation or a blistering battle. I remember feeling my heart race as I approached the Paradise door, uncertain about what to expect. My eyes, as I walked in and adjusted to the darkness, were drawn to you sitting on your familiar stool at the far end of the smoke-filled bar; and I responded immediately to your familiar gesture, motioning me to your side. Amidst the noise and confusion—orders being called out from the kitchen and people joining foursomes or sixsomes already feeling the effects of a few drinks—you had noticed me. Even with the dim lighting, I could see as I drew nearer to you that your skin had a kind of grayish hue. Your eyes seemed to be so hollowed and darkened. I wondered whether you were overly tired or overly worked, still unable to comprehend how this illness had taken hold. I hadn't seen you for a while, as I mentioned, and it saddened me to see you like this. I suggested that we sit at a table for some privacy and observed that you needed a cane for support as we walked those few steps. You were so thin, perhaps 120 pounds, not much more. The anger and fear that consumed me before I stepped inside the bar were so quickly replaced with a kind of tenderness, a need to comfort you in some way, rather than to confront you as I had planned with our more usual talks about child support so long overdue. That is why I began talking about the children and how they were all doing, how beautiful your new granddaughter was, and asking you about your family. That is also why I invited you to our home to see Shiloh the following Sunday afternoon.

I remember my pulling out a cigarette to calm my nerves and your reaching for a match to light it for me, a gesture that drew me back in an instant to those wonderful college days when we first met. We had fun making small talk again that day, laughing the way we used to laugh, telling the familiar stories that braided our lives together; and I saw once more that handsome, broad smile of yours that used to melt my heart so long ago. I didn't let on that I was worried about you. If you had said that you wanted to make one more try with me, I know that I would have accepted—but for the wrong reasons. You didn't, of course. You did say something about my not needing to worry about money and that it would come, which didn't really make sense at that moment as we were barely getting by from week to week. The only thing that made sense was that secret part of me that still wanted to stay, but too soon it was time to go.

I already had stayed more than an hour, much longer than planned. You stood up like a gentleman as I rose to leave and asked once more for a hug, embracing me as if you would never have the chance again. I felt myself surrendering, sinking into your arms, closing my eyes, being in the moment, and wanting time miraculously to stop—right there. You gave me a long, tender kiss on the cheek, pulled your head back to look into my eyes, and slowly—reluctantly—began to release me. First, you stepped back ever so slightly, allowing your hands to move and caress my shoulders. Then while giving them a gentle squeeze—a tender smile with lips closed appeared on your face, a single nod of your forehead told me to step back, and finally you let go. Oh, John, I know now that you were saying good-bye.

You came to see Lars and your granddaughter, Shiloh, a few days later. I still remember that magical moment when you first arrived, an instant etched in my memory with so many others of the good times we shared. As you came in to say hello, you extended your hand toward mine. I reached out to you as well, and for a split second, our fingers touched. My cheeks flushed. Our hands without instruction then moved more comfortably apart, but the image of that momentary connection hung sweetly in the air. Without an audience of children, perhaps I would have kissed you; but instead—after that barely perceptible pause—we began polite conversation. We had, after all, already said good-bye.

The children and I felt a bit awkward, and you were clearly not feeling your best. We all seemed to feel lumps in our throats of wishes that would not release themselves from the that familiar world of "if only." None of us knew how to translate into words our wishes for the life we could no longer have, the desire to be a family once more; yet the sub-text was there behind every glance, every smile, every expression. So certain were we that we had let that dream go, only to feel it rebound with this precious newborn in our midst. I know you so well, John, and could see the discomfort that you were feeling. You worked so hard to hold back your tears, finally leaving before any pride was lost. We agreed as I walked you back to your car that we would work together to resolve our financial differences. You said quietly, "I'll call you," and that was it—our final conversation.

The kids and I sent pictures of you holding the baby in your arms, along with the usual Valentine's Day cards. Two weeks later, Kristin met you as she always did for your birthday lunch—where else but at the Paradise Lounge? We were enjoying the changes in Shiloh, realizing with each passing day what a blessing she was to us all—someone so innocent to love and to cherish. Kristin surprised us with a mid-week visit from campus on March 2, needing to use our VCR for a class project. Her infrequent appearances were always a delight, giving us all a chance to catch up on everything from her school to my business and, of course, to her brothers and niece. The house became quiet when Lars took the baby to settle her down for the night. I finished straightening up the kitchen and then went to bed, while Kristin watched her assigned video in the family room. Nels was visiting a friend that night. None of us expected a phone call. Our once tranquil, peaceful home was about to explode.

It was about 10:00 P.M. The phone rang twice, and Lars answered it.

"It's for you, mom," he yelled from his room.

"That's strange," I thought. "I never get phone calls in the evening," I said to myself feeling rather perplexed. I picked up the phone in my room. "Yes, this is she," I answered.

"I'm calling from the Dane County Coroner's Office," the voice on the phone explained. "We've been looking for Kristin Forde since 7:00 P.M. and wondered if she were there," he said. "What," I wondered, "would they want her for?" And then I replied, "She's here," but then, thinking the worst, asked, "It's not my son, is it?"

"No. We found your former husband in his apartment this evening, and he's dead."

"What do you mean?" I asked, absolutely unable to process what I had just heard. "Are you sure? I mean are you sure it's John?" I stumbled, not knowing what to say, what to do. "How did you find out?" I questioned, knowing that you lived alone.

He explained that the police had responded to a call of concern from one of your friends after he missed you for a pre-arranged meeting. When there was no answer, he phoned the police who unlocked your door, and . . . . there was your body already cold on the floor.

Suddenly I knew I had to be there. I never rehearsed this scene in my mind before, not this one. I just needed to be where you had lived your last hours, and I knew the kids would want to be there, too. "Can we come down to the apartment? I think we have to be there, please, if it would be possible."

"No problem, ma'am. How soon can you be here?" he asked.

"We'll come as soon as we can." I managed to say, "Thank you," barely able to believe any of what I had heard. Tears and sobs began to take control of my body, but before I gave into the need to let go, I grabbed onto my head thinking, "I have to get myself together. I have to get Nels." I phoned a neighbor who agreed to pick him up, after explaining that the children's father had died. "Where is Kristin?" I wondered. "Oh, she's watching her video downstairs. I have to tell her first," I determined.

Then I began what was for me the most difficult part of all. I knew that the task of telling the children was mine alone. I also knew how much they loved you, needed you, admired you, no matter what your and my differences were. I was about to tell them that they would never be able to share special times, take trips to the farm, walk and talk with you again. Even knowing this, I underestimated the depth of grief they would feel. "How do I do this?" I asked myself. "Please, dear God, tell me what to say." I searched for words that might more gently ease them into the next phase of their young lives, one without a father to love. Kristin was the first, and she nearly erupted both physically and emotionally, so grief-stricken that she was convinced she herself would not survive. I tried to hold her to console her, but found myself unprepared for the intensity of her heartbreak. Lars was the second, coming into a room already flowing with tears, bending to the floor to cry and to conceal his pain. Nels arrived minutes later. Our neighbor broke the news to him while they were in the driveway. He joined us as we all held each other, crying first, and finally agreeing that we each needed to call friends. "It can't be happening," I thought. "I'll never make it. I can't manage this. What am I supposed to be doing?"

The next hours were total chaos, filled with tears and a pain that would not—never did—go away. Not until the next day did we know it was suicide, some kind of prescription sleeping pills. We went down to your apartment that night to be where you had spent your last hours, hoping perhaps for some kind of explanation or understanding or comforting experience. We all needed to be there to feel your presence somehow. We saw the place where you evidently had fallen, letters from me and birthday cards from the children scattered on the floor, as well as a note of instructions that you had left for us. No one cried. We were in too much shock. The children gently touched your belongings, picked up a pen you may have just used, reached out for a favorite sweater and coat to hold close just one more time. I did the same after they left, praying silently for you and for all of us left behind. We had so much more to go through with the funeral and were just beginning to face that reality. I needed strength.

The children loved you, John, more than you will ever know. They planned most of the funeral, which included the recording made years ago of you singing "Ol' Man River." They shed so many tears for you, as those present that day shed tears for all of us.

So many difficult things happened at this already difficult time, producing more rage and pain, more sadness and grief. I was incredulous when both the apartment manager and leasing agency sent me bills for money you owed them, and again when another friend of yours asked me about your insurance, to be sure that he wouldn't get stuck with a note he had co-signed. Within days, I faced the terrifying reality of my divorce lawyer's failure to protect me from bankruptcy and all of the fallout that it entailed. I had trusted her completely with my future and the futures of our children, never imagining that she would overlook critical details in my settlement, such as a life insurance policy for you. Comments from other people in attendance about how lonely you had been seemed to imply that somehow I was responsible for this. Maybe I was overly sensitive or feeling guilty. No one who knew our life's story could possibly have had any thoughts of the kind. Thank heavens for those who did remind me of what I had done, what I had tried to do, and how impossible it is for anyone to gain power over another's alcoholism.

The funeral itself might have pleased you, as there were many mourners there from all walks of your life, including the Governor, your lobbying colleagues, and your friends from the Paradise Lounge. Most could think of little to say to me or to the children. Clearly, they were grief-stricken for you and for all of us. Perhaps they were unaware of the extent of your illness, were unprepared for your sudden death, or were unwilling to acknowledge what they may have known or feared all along. I had not really thought about the vast number of people who knew a part of you; and the image of all of them there that day—many of whom I had never even met—still confuses me. What did they mean to you and you to them?

I was glad that Pastor Klyve included alcoholism in his sermon, which let it be known to all who were present that your death was tragic but that you had brought it on yourself. The children needed to hear that message. They had such a hard time letting you go. They did help distribute your ashes, according to your wishes, on both your father's grave and the Mississippi River. What you'd think about the plaque in your memory that hangs on the wall at the Paradise Lounge, I could not venture to guess. To me, it seems more than a bit of a paradox—celebrating your life in the very place where you literally drank yourself to death. They must have seen it coming. Did the Paradise Lounge bring you the paradise you wanted? Like so many other questions, I wish I had an answer to that one. It might make it easier for us to go on without you.

John, I have continued to live my life, but I wish you knew how hard it still is for me to smile. Freeing myself from those all-consuming feelings and recurrent nightmares that pull me down is taking longer than I expected. Maybe that means that I don't want to let you go. I really don't know. It is different for the children, it seems. They cherish your memory, almost seeming afraid at times that they will forget you, your face, your voice. Kristin always wears the silver necklace you gave her; and Nels, your ring. For Lars, it is your English-styled riding hat. I, of course, have put my remembrances of you away. Seeing those one-time treasures now brings me pain rather than comfort. I am trying to forgive you, John, not just for your benefit but for mine as well. And I must forgive myself, too, as I accept responsibility for my own life and the choices that I made. Yes, my "overs" list is rather long, as yours must be. I just don't want to add anything else to it.

You may ask why it took me so long to write these letters. I could not have written them even a year ago. I was still living the nightmare. Good friends have helped me get past it all. So, too, has my therapist. It was her idea, in fact, that I try to write it all down, all that has been locked up inside me and kept me from moving on. In writing these letters to you, I have begun to sort out everything, to reflect on it all, and to add a perspective that only time makes possible. You can't write back; but I knew you so well, John, that I can almost hear the words you'd want to write. You'd tell me and the children again, as you did in your last note that last night, "I love you." You would ask us all not to look back in sadness but to look ahead at the promise the future holds. I hope you're right about that. It is a tough order to follow, but we will try. . . . .

Once upon a time, I knew a handsome young man from a small farming town near the Mississippi River. He attended a one-room country school as a child, earned the pride of his community as both a scholar and a musician, and became the joy of his family as their beloved and only son. I knew the man with the soothing baritone voice and a heart of gold who sang me beautiful love songs in college and wrote me tender love letters from overseas. He escorted me to fraternity formals, taught me how to ride a horse, made me laugh, brought me flowers, fulfilled my every dream. He was the grandson of strong immigrant Norwegians, a man who became my first love, then my husband, and finally the father of my children. He was an accomplished man of wit and wisdom. . . . *He was a gentleman, a romantic, fun, intelligent, a lover of good music and off-the-road restaurants, a reader of popular novels and newsy periodicals; and he was attracted to me. . . .* This is the John whom I see every day in the faces of Kristin, Nels, and Lars. This is the John whom I want to remember, the one who died so long ago.

And now the time has come, my dearest John, for *me* to say good-bye.

ja elska da,

Catherine

June 18, 1997

Ft. Leonard Wood, Mo.
Nov. 5, 1966

Dear Cathy,

. . . . .Sounds like things are going well in Madison. I'm glad you're keeping busy- Renny's girl* and everything. You're really ambitious. If you have access to a camera, I'd really like to see your paintings and sculptures- keep it in mind.

The training is getting tougher already- I almost died yesterday-my arms are still sore from all the pushups, but I'm already getting in better shape . . . The barracks tonight are not prison walls-but a place of relaxation-an example of Gibran's "appearance of things changing with emotions!". . . .

. . . . .Some quotes from Gibran that give me a lot of comfort here at good ol' Ft. Lost in the Woods:. . .

"To steal a flower, we call mean. To rob a field is chivalry."

"Who kills the body, he must die. Who kills the spirit he goes free."

---

* "Renny's girl" was the name given to the women who worked at any of Madison's famous Rennebohm Drug stores.

"Man cannot reap love until after sad and revealing separation, and bitter patience, and desperate hardship."!. . .

"The most beautiful thing in life is that our souls remain hovering over the places where we once enjoyed ourselves."

One more—"The appearance of things changes according to the emotions, and thus we see magic and beauty in them, while the magic and beauty are really in ourselves.". . . .

John

PART II

LESSONS LEARNED

CHAPTER 6

A 12-STEP PROGRAM FOR PARTNERS & COUNSELORS

Dear Reader:

My gift to you is my life, one that admittedly has been far from "picture perfect," but one from which I have learned a great deal. The process of writing my journal clarified my memories of a treasured relationship that did not survive. Our children are all that remain of that once-magical bond. I expected so much more from life, of course. I wanted to grow old with someone who knew and loved me then and now. That someone was John, and that's someone whom I will never have again. I needed to understand this, to grieve the loss, and then to move on. Finally I did as I put my thoughts on paper.

Initially, I wrote as a release, but as Mary transposed my private journal into letters to John, I began to see options that I completely overlooked at the time. What follows here are those revelations. My only regret is that a simple list such as this—written for the partner (like me) rather than the alcoholic—was not available years ago. I needed practical ideas rather than co-dependence guilt, just as I needed some acknowledgment for the complexity of my dilemma. Subsequent conversations with Mary led to these "12 steps," which we now share with hopes that others who read them will find courage to act—while there is still time.

PART I: THE EDUCATION PHASE (BECOME YOUR OWN EXPERT.)

Step One. Get statistics on alcoholism. *Discover that you are not alone.* It helped me immensely to know that I was not the only person living with an alcoholic. I found a strange comfort in realizing that my feelings were echoed by so many others, and this helped me focus on finding some kind of solution with which I could live. You will need to borrow or purchase at least one good resource book on alcoholism, covering topics such as its frequency, causes, consequences, and cures. Like me, you may be surprised to learn that almost 20 million people in the United States have a serious drinking problem, 5 million of whom are teenagers. I was stunned to read that alcohol abuse accounts for 100,000 deaths annually in our country alone, including 50% of our automobile fatalities! These data will convince you that you are literally among millions whose lives are compromised by a partner's addiction. You also may be convinced that now is a good time to get your life in order.

I began my attempt to acquire an education 25 years too late. In my defense, programs for alcoholics and their partners or families were relatively unknown to most of us in the early 1970s. The results of not knowing what to do or where to start were catastrophic in my case. My marriage could no longer be rescued. My subsequent divorce left me penniless, and John's debts—which became mine after his death—prevent me even now from living beyond a subsistence level. Death—whether it happens as a result of illness, accident, or suicide—solves matters only for the deceased. The living must bear the weight of those unresolved matters for their lifetimes. While financial issues are often temporary, emotional scars are permanent. I cannot overemphasize how important it is to start reading and preparing today for what will happen tomorrow.

Step Two. Understand the causes of addiction. *Know the reasons behind the behavior.* Knowing why your partner is addicted will help you to see it less as a personality trait and more as an illness. Rather than *guess* at causes, ask. When you ask, listen. When you listen, listen to gain an understanding rather than to teach or to preach. If your partner is like John, you will discover that it will take more than one conversation to gather the information that you need; and you may need the help of a counselor, therapist, or physician to complete this learning task. Once the cause is known (for example, depression, anxiety, or habit), a professional will know how to intervene. The solution process (according to my counselor) cannot begin without knowing the problem's cause. It really cannot begin at all without a conversation. I wish that someone had told me this. It seems so obvious now, yet John and I never discussed his reasons for drinking.

Actually, my therapist explained to me that people drink for different reasons. I recently read in *Newsweek* magazine (September 8, 1997) that some individuals may be genetically predisposed to becoming alcoholic, just as others have family histories that place them at risk for heart disease. In these cases, life needs to be lived with more caution. Limiting alcohol can diminish the power of alcohol genes in the same way that for some, limiting one's cholesterol intake can reduce the likelihood of a heart attack. A genetic tendency, in other words, is not a death sentence, unless one chooses to ignore it. Others, like John, acquire the drinking habit to cope with psychological problems such as shyness, anxiety, fear, insomnia, depression, rage, or lack of self-esteem. The unfortunate truth is that alcohol is often effective in relieving the symptoms related to these conditions. Those who treat alcoholics have found that shy people who have a glass of wine, for example, become more comfortable among strangers. Anxious people may become calm after one or two beers. And a few drinks can produce a temporary high for those experiencing a mild depression. In fact, for those who truly do manage their alcohol intake and who acknowledge both the cognitive and the physiological limitations when under its influence, controlled drinking makes sense, at least to me. For the alcoholic like John who neither manages drinking nor acknowledges limitations with any degree of reliability, soothing these kinds of problems with alcohol makes about as much sense as watering your garden with a fire hose.

John appears to have used alcohol to overcome anxiety, as closely as I can tell; but his illness was far more complex than that. He was a country boy with superior intellectual ability. He found himself first in a college fraternity with more worldly and equally gifted peers and later among power brokers with three-piece suits and cigars. In each of these venues, drinking came as part of the culture; but John never acquired those essential alcohol-management skills that might have prevented his habit from becoming an addiction and eventually an illness. Moreover, on those few occasions when I brought the problem to his attention, he refused to believe that he had a drinking problem and tragically gave up his will to live rather than face his world as one who didn't have all of the answers after all.

Curiously, John was never more well-liked or successful than he was when he was sober. I learned the hard way that success will not persuade the alcoholic to quit drinking when the underlying cause for that behavior has not been addressed. John felt better when he drank, and thus he continued to drink. That is why I believe that lasting solutions to alcoholism must focus on causes, not just behaviors. The discomfort that the alcoholic experiences is real. Telling an alcoholic to stop drinking, without acknowledging either the problem source or the pain it produces and without offering a reasonable alternative, is a bit like telling a non-swimmer to remove his life jacket before jumping into the lake. Alcoholics are smarter than that, and John is a case in point.

Step Three. Determine whether your partner *needs* alcohol. *"Need" identifies an addict.* Needing alcohol is neither normal nor healthy. You may recall that I grew up in a social context surrounded by alcohol. Practically all family acquaintances and many family members began their drinking for social and business reasons. I assumed that drinking was an activity that naturally came along with success. The drinking-success connection, in fact, appeared normal to me. I mistook my father's alcohol need, for example, as his reward for having survived another tough day at the office. Alcohol appeared to me as a badge of achievement, a rite of passage, probably eclipsing any concern I might have developed for John's drinking during our early years together. Moreover, John actually was more fun when he drank, whereas he was anxious and tense when sober. Thus, I offered no resistance when drinking became part of our normal evening routine. John, however, did not just want alcohol. He *needed* it. *Need,* according to my reading of the literature, is a major determining factor in making the alcoholism diagnosis. And *needing* to have many drinks on a daily basis is simply not normal, healthy behavior.

True, some people drink during social events without ever becoming alcoholics. Others, on the advice of their physicians, drink a glass of wine each day to reduce the dangers of heart disease. Still others are instructed in controlled-drinking strategies with a definite measure of success. In these cases, the drinker's body does not beg for alcohol. Should prohibition return, casual and controlled drinkers surely would miss it. Missing is not needing, however. Missing is wanting, and there is a big difference between the two. I believe that the difference is captured best by the word "addiction."

Alcoholics like John who go without their drinks often exhibit physical signs of distress that tell them that their body needs a drink. They become uncomfortable, nervous, restless, and panicky. Their hands tremble, eyes look anxious, breathing is more rapid, and speech becomes intense, if not explosive. John followed that response pattern precisely. Only too late did I learn that these visible symptoms were evidence of an alcohol-dependent (addicted) body. I have learned that alcohol for him was like insulin to the diabetic, returning his body to a state of calm almost immediately. To avoid the unpleasant effects associated with alcohol withdrawal, John managed his environment in clever ways such as: (1) taking jobs where alcohol is part of the culture; (2) meeting clients at bars; (3) acquiring a circle of drinking friends; (4) attending only those social engagements where alcohol is available; (5) gravitating to group activities where drinking is center stage; (6) bringing a bottle to work; (7) taking a personal liquor cabinet on vacations; (8) having a bottle under the seat in the car; and (9) keeping his habit a secret. The alcoholic *needs* to do many of these things and *needs* to drink on a regular basis. None of these life-style adjustments by itself necessarily signals a need. Taken together, however, one has just cause for concern. I wish that I had known this earlier.

Concern on your part should become alarm when drinking causes a change in personality, frequent passing out, physical aggression, belligerence, the destruction of property, the accumulation of DWI's and associated fines, or regular embarrassment from public displays of inappropriate behavior. These behaviors may become the norm for the alcoholic who drinks to reduce such feelings as anxiety or depression. Needing to drink to this degree is evidence of a serious health problem, one that calls for intervention. I ignored all of these indicators, preferring the Scarlet O'Hara strategy of thinking about it tomorrow. I became absorbed in child-rearing and community fund-raising as socially accepted alternatives. I actually remember thinking that my faith in God would make John's problem behaviors go away. You'd be hard pressed to find a more resolute wishful-thinker.

Step Four. Know the health risks associated with alcohol abuse. *Be prepared to act.* Again, most books on the topic cover all significant medical conditions to which an alcoholic may succumb. The reason to understand these health consequences is both to face the grim possibility of what may follow if intervention comes too late and to acquire the courage needed to confront that reality. In other words, alcohol will do more than temporarily impair vision or hamper mental judgment. In time, it will cause permanent, irreversible damage to critical body organs and to the nervous system, while often leading its user down a path to an early death. Partners wanting to avert these consequences will need to take some kind of action.

Initially, I must admit that I was unaware of how catastrophic these health consequences were. My own family circle hid both alcoholism and its effects for decades. Not until I attended the NewStart program for families of alcoholics did I acquire the knowledge that I needed to comprehend the severity of John's illness. Aided by a concerned employer and armed with NewStart's information on addiction, I found the courage to confront John and to get him into treatment. He was a resistant patient during the first intervention but compliant the second time around. He found the motivation to make it work when his employer demanded sobriety. For nearly four years, he seemed to be a "success story." We all believed that, for John, alcohol was a matter of history!

Unfortunately, recovery began too late. John's entire adult life had centered on drinking. Without alcohol, life lost its meaning, its joy, its cohesive structure. The pull back to alcohol eventually overpowered him. Having information about alcoholism and addiction 15 years earlier—before his drinking became a need and an integral part of his daily routine—might have saved our marriage and possibly John's life.

Step Five. Recognize that recovery requires medical treatment. *Recovery itself can be life-threatening.* I was surprised to learn this fact from NewStart, never realizing that an alcoholic actually could die if alcohol intake is terminated abruptly. For this reason, physicians do not recommend that alcoholics undertake recovery efforts without medical assistance. Like cancer, alcoholism will most likely get worse without treatment. Moreover, the sooner caught, the greater the chance for a cure. It is not prudent to wait as I did and to pray for miracles. It is best to seek help from professionals well-trained for this particular disease.

Medical treatment will probably include a wide range of recommendations from diet, exercise, and basic education to inpatient treatment, medication, and therapy. Solutions are neither immediate nor simple, but I can attest to the fact that they *can* work. Your biggest problem (and mine), of course, will be in getting the cooperation of your partner to accept treatment. Most will reject the belief that they drink too much or the perception that they have a drinking problem. Like John, they may become abusive when such suggestions are made. They may be more inclined to listen, however, if you have the support of friends, family, and employers (see Step 7) who can confirm your observations. John was not willing to listen to me, but he was willing to listen to his boss. He was even more willing when I ceased all of my enabling behaviors.

Step Six. Understand that behavioral changes come from within. *Your power to change another person is limited.* It is best to face the fact that people change because *they* want to change—not simply because someone else wants them to do so. This was so hard for me to accept. The alcoholic in your midst may never change, but always remember that you are only responsible for your own behavior. You will want to make the commitment to change yourself when you realize that you cannot co-exist with someone whose behavior demands that you alter yours to compensate and to camouflage simply to survive. I reached the end of my rope before I sought help because I feared the consequences, feared the unknown. Believe me, I know how disabling fear can be.

That is why it is important to ask yourself two important questions: (1) To what extent are my behaviors feeding my partner's addiction? and (2) To what extent is our relationship dependent upon alcohol? Many relationships actually become alcohol-dependent, with partners forgetting how to relate to each other when they are sober. In other cases, partners enjoy drinking (as I did) and see no reason to give it up. Still others contribute to their partner's stress or depression through antagonizing behaviors, giving the alcoholic more reason to "self-medicate" when they are together. The moral here is that the alcoholic does not exist in a vacuum. The dynamics of the marriage relationship itself may be the problem, with alcohol abuse being merely a symptom of that larger concern. In this case, marriage counseling or divorce planning may make more sense. A good counselor will help you make that decision.

Although you cannot demand change, a change in your behavior has the potential to produce change in your partner as a natural consequence. The process is somewhat parallel to shifting positions in a canoe, where one person's move causes another to make an adjustment to maintain stability. For example, you can refuse to be driven home by an alcoholic partner, driving yourself or taking a taxi instead. You can decline invitations to social engagements where alcohol is served, telling the host that your partner's alcohol consumption is a problem for you. You can be honest with the boss, friends, and family members when drinking interferes with the alcoholic's performance, a strategy that will appear less hostile with a warning of your intention to do so. You can insist that your home is an "alcohol-free zone." Minor changes such as these could give you control of some parts of your life, while also reducing the frequency of life-threatening circumstances or embarrassing social situations. You will also be sending your partner a message: "I do not want a life controlled by alcohol." I can see now in retrospect that I passed up many opportunities to take similar action.

The effort to produce a healthy home environment, one where change can occur, will prompt you to consider causes for addiction (Step 2) and alternative solutions. Start by finding safer ways, for example, to reduce stress (*i.e.*, exercise, massage, tennis, or saying "no" to speaking engagements). You may want to suggest counseling for depression (and possibly medication). It probably would be a good idea to introduce new social activities that do not require liquor (*i.e.*, going to plays, to movies, or to Little League games). Try arranging to be with non-drinking friends for alcohol-free social activities (a "breakfast club" before work or on weekends). Bad habits need to be replaced by healthy habits—*one at a time*. The alternatives you suggest may be flatly rejected, but you will find peace in knowing that you have made a sincere attempt to ease the transition to a sober life. Moreover, nothing should prevent *you* from changing *your* recreational activities, a move that will offer you the beginnings of a new life regardless of your partner's choice. Yes, I know: This takes courage.

Some may need to send an even more powerful message to get the results (specifically, the safety) that you deserve. You may need to move out of your home, to file for divorce, or to call 911 to arrange for a police escort to a detoxification center. These kinds of actions are necessary when situations become hostile and life-threatening. True: These kinds of decisions may set in motion feared consequences, including divorce. Clearly, there is no guarantee that your relationship will survive. You may find that the hurt is too deep to be forgiven, that alcohol is too important to live without, or that trust simply cannot be restored, even when sobriety is achieved. You may discover that you have grown apart emotionally. Others may find new mates who are more compatible. These are the kinds of injuries and consequences for which alcoholism is infamous. They are the same injuries that early efforts to produce a changed environment might prevent.

PART II: THE ACTION PHASE (TAKE RESPONSIBILITY FOR YOURSELF.)

Step Seven. Go public by creating a support team. *Confronting an alcoholic is more easily accomplished with the help of others who care.* Defeating alcoholism calls for the support of key individuals in all areas of the alcoholic's world: home, work, and social life included. You must let these individuals know your concern with the hope that they will support, rather than sabotage, your efforts. Believe me when I say that this takes courage. Your knowledge about the causes and consequences of alcoholism will serve you well in these conversations. Then go public one step further by asking your partner to arrange for a professional assessment and diagnosis. You may enlist the help of the alcoholic's employer, who agrees to make this medical check-up a condition of work. That was the only way that I could get John to comply. The more courageous reader may also make the check-up a condition for your continuing in the relationship.

The importance of seeking medical confirmation is critical. In a best-case scenario, you will discover that your concerns are unwarranted. On the other hand, there is the possibility that the symptoms you observe stem from an even more serious medical problem such as a brain tumor or multiple sclerosis. In other words, don't jump to conclusions. Advice from a medical doctor often is taken more seriously than similar recommendations from a partner. In addition, the physician can make immediate referrals to other specialists, including therapists or inpatient treatment centers. Remember: It is beyond your power to insist that your partner see a physician or that any recommended treatment is followed. Your role is to make resources available, to provide encouragement, and then to go on with your life if help and advice are rejected.

To this day, I regret not having discussed John's drinking with anyone. I can see now that I lost opportunities to receive help from family and friends, some of whom still hold resentments for having been left out of the communication loop. I carried the additional burden of making up excuses to cover for John missing work, choir practice, and family reunions where his absences raised suspicions. I gave up valuable time trying to project the right image, time that would have been better spent preparing for my future. I ended up fighting the battle with an army of one—myself alone. Again, going public takes courage.

Others will know that your life is not perfect, that your partner is not perfect, and that you are perfectly helpless without the support of everyone. As difficult as that seems to admit, imagine admitting at a later date to your deception (Step Eight) and imagine everyone telling you that they knew the truth all along. That's what I did. Please believe me when I tell you that those consequences are far worse.

Step Eight. Terminate all "cover up" activities. *Be honest with family, friends, and people in the workplace.* Understand the destructive power of deceit. Put simply: *Never lie* to family, friends, co-workers, bosses, strangers; and, most important, never lie to yourself! Lying may seem easier than admitting the truth, but the price tag is enormous. It includes losing valuable friendships, losing your own credibility, and alienating family members who feel rejected by your refusal to tell them precisely what is going on. Don't tell the boss that your partner has a touch of the flu if the truth is that he has a hangover. Don't tell friends that your partner had to stay late at the office if the truth is that the "office" is a nearby bar. Don't tell relatives that a scheduling conflict prevents you from attending the reunion if the truth is that you are terrified your partner will get too drunk or that the two of you are not getting along because of his drinking behavior. Don't lie to yourself by saying that you have averted another embarrassing moment, when the truth is that you have enabled your partner one more time. This was my primary mistake, an enabling pattern that takes on a life of its own as one lie grooms the path for another and another.

Telling the truth will feel right, especially if you discuss your intention to do so with your partner in advance. Make it understood that you will no longer cover up the disease (a change in your behavior that may produce a change in his or hers!). Remember that most people recognize dishonesty for what it is anyway. They either will pity the liar as one who is too weak to behave responsibly, or they will feel hurt in realizing that you have no confidence in their ability to understand. Simply stated, lying and denying destroy relationships, while reinforcing addiction. If you have any doubt about this, reread my story before continuing. Believe me: I know that "simple" doesn't make it easy.

Step Nine. Listen to those who care. *Pay attention when others tell you that they are concerned about your partner's drinking.* Occasionally, friends or family will express their concerns for your partner's drinking. Several of my closest, most trusted friends, did try to speak with me about John's behavior. My only explanation for ignoring them is that I was not ready to listen or to admit that his drinking was out of control. Don't make the same mistake. Remember that it takes a great deal of courage to be the bearer of bad news or to ask the embarrassing question. Someone who has mustered the courage to talk deserves to have an audience. Moreover, one cannot expect friends to remain sympathetic when their concerns are rejected. Rather than make excuses, find the courage to listen and to trust. These are the people, after all, who are saying that they want to be there for you.

Think back now to friends or family members who may have tried to open up this conversation before you were prepared to listen, much less to act. They are the people to call first. Pick up the phone and begin with an apology, which may reopen that door. Trust that true friends and caring family members will understand. Most will be grateful that once again you trust and value them. They may be waiting and hoping to hear from you now.

Step Ten. Support a recovering alcoholic. *Note the difference between taking responsibility for another's behavior and acting responsibly yourself.* Understand that a recovering alcoholic is still an alcoholic. It took me too long to understand this. Actually, I do not remember anyone ever telling me that John would need my help for many years to come. Alcoholics who emerge from treatment are vulnerable, and they may remain vulnerable for a very long time. Ideally, they should return to an alcohol-free environment—both at home and at work—to reduce temptation and to establish new, healthy behavior patterns. John was a lobbyist, a profession where drinking is a tool of the trade, or so he claimed. It would have been prudent, perhaps, for him to change careers entirely or to move within his agency to a less alcohol-demanding position. It would have been nice if a non-drinking peer were willing to accompany him on trips out of town so that he had someone to be with to fill the lonely hours. I might have insisted on traveling with him, if no one else were available. The trips to Reno and to Norway are cases in point here, for each was associated with relapses that may have been avoided. There is no reason to take unnecessary chances when an alcoholic is most at risk, during those early years of recovery from the disease. There is a difference, of course, between taking responsibility for the alcoholic's behavior and a partner's behaving responsibly. The alcoholic must maintain a commitment to sobriety, while the partner supports those efforts to the extent possible.

Step Eleven. Avoid the blaming and the "if only" games. *Do not externalize the cause of addiction or waste time dwelling on past decisions.* If you are like me and discover that your partner is an alcoholic, you will try to figure out *who* or *what* caused it and what *you* might have done differently to have avoided it altogether. What I learned from my reading is that this kind of thinking is actually very common. As hard as it is to believe, however, people don't *cause* others to become alcoholics. Neither do psychological conditions such as depression or traumatic events such as loss of employment have the power to *cause* someone to drink. I spent years wondering what I did, what John's mother did, what happened in Vietnam, and what his employers did to make John an alcoholic. My reading helped me understand the hard truth, that the alcoholic is responsible for becoming an alcoholic.

Another kind of thinking is fantasizing about how different life *would* have been "*if only* I had realized this was serious" or "*if only* I had married someone else." In my case, it was easier to think about what I *might* have done than it was to think about what I *should* be doing. You will resist these kinds of fruitless mental exercises more easily once you start reading and learning. You will begin slowly to refocus your energy toward what you can do now rather than on what you may have done in the past. I must confess that I still fall back into this kind of thinking from time to time. Perhaps I always will. It never makes me feel any better, however, and that is why I now try to interrupt that line of thinking as soon as it starts. I am getting better, and you will, too.

This is my advice: Don't blame anyone, including yourself, for making your partner an alcoholic. Accept responsibility for your own actions and past decisions, but then move on. The simple truth is that the alcoholic *chooses* alcohol. No life circumstance, no personal problem, no genetic predisposition brings glory to that choice. No mother's neglect, no father's belt, no loss of job, no stock market drop, has the power to force that decision—not without the alcoholic's consent. It has taken me too many years to finally understand this. I always believed that I could make John stop drinking, and even worse, I blamed myself for failing. I know now that I was powerless from the start to change him.

Step Twelve. Promise yourself a better life. *And act on that promise!* The perfect ending to this journey would include a relationship intact and sobriety forever. The alcoholic, unfortunately, may have caused too much damage, inflicted too much pain, and destroyed your faith, while stunting his/her own emotional growth and development. Some alcoholics with fears of divorce, death, loss of health, or loss of career become motivated to seek help. Others, like John, are too far gone even to entertain the possibility of change. Remember: Alcoholics may choose to continue drinking; but you can choose a better life—one free from heartbreak, one free from alcohol.

The decision to change is a decision that you make for *your* life with the hope that your partner will join you in your own "recovery." Expect that decision to bring relief, but trepidation as well; for even good changes bring you to unfamiliar territory. You will be rejoining a society that you left years ago, and people may not know how to react to your presence. They may not know the person you have become, the one who can finally live and love again. Reconnecting and re-establishing meaningful relationships will take time. You will need that time for your own personal growth and emotional development, just as others will need that time to make room in their lives for you again. I promise you, it will happen; and I know that I am not an exception in this regard.

Don't wait as long as I did to take the first step. Don't let this disease steal one more day from you. Begin now by learning all that you can learn about alcoholism. You will acquire courage as you acquire knowledge. With knowledge, courage, and the support of family and friends, you can make the commitment to change; and you will be able to act. Soon you will experience a normal, healthy life again—one that is free of embarrassment and fear, that is predictable and fulfilling. My life and John's illustrate one simple lesson: Alcoholism cannot take your life without your permission. Our lives will have a positive legacy after all, if this book becomes your catalyst.

Thank you for walking with me through my life's journey. Trust that in spirit I will walk with you now as you begin yours!

Sincerely,